GLOBETROTTER™

T

C000175500

SRI LANKA

Robin Gauldie

NEW
HOLLAND

NEW
HOLLAND

★★★ Highly recommended
★★ Recommended
★ See if you can

Sixth edition published in 2015
by MapStudio™
10 9 8 7 6 5 4 3 2 1
www.globetrottertravelguides.com

Distributed in Africa by
MapStudio™
Unit 3, Block B, M5 Park, Eastman Road,
Maitland 7405, Cape Town, South Africa
PO Box 193, Maitland 7404

Distributed in the UK/Europe/Asia by
John Beaufoy Publishing Ltd

Distributed in the USA by
National Book Network

ISBN 978 1 77026 684 1

This guidebook has been written by independent authors and
updaters. The information therein represents their impartial
opinion, and neither they nor the publishers accept payment
in return for including in the book or writing more favourable
reviews of any of the establishments. Whilst every effort has
been made to ensure that this guidebook is as accurate and
up to date as possible, please be aware that the facts quoted
are subject to change, particularly the price of food, transport
and accommodation. The Publisher accepts no responsibility
or liability for any loss, injury or inconvenience incurred by
readers or travellers using this guide.

Commissioning Editor: Elaine Fick
DTP Cartographic Manager: Genené Hart
Editors: Elaine Fick, Thea Grobbelaar, Carla Redelinghuys,
Nicky Steenkamp, Melany Porter, Mary Duncan, Sara Harper
Picture Researchers: Shavonne Govender, Carmen
Hartzenberg, Colette Stott
Design and DTP: Nicole Bannister, Michael Lyons
Cartographers: Rudi de Lange, Genené Hart, Lorissa
Bouwer, Marisa Roman, Carl Germishuys

Reproduction by Hirt & Carter (Pty) Ltd, Cape Town
Printed and bound by Craft Print International Ltd, Singapore

Photographic Credits:
Peter Adams/awl-images.com: pages 108, 114; Will Gray/
awl-images.com: page 10; Paul Harris/awl-images.com:
page 81; Amar Grover/awl-images.com: page 16; Gavin
Hellier/awl-images.com: title page, pages 4, 6; Rob Penn/
awl-images.com: page 17; Travel Pix Collection/awl-images.
com: pages 23, 28, 54; Ian Trower/awl-images.com: page 12;
Gerald Cubitt: pages 46, 56, 58, 80; Caroline Jones: pages
68, 84; Jeanetta Baker/PhotoBank: page 20; Peter Baker/
PhotoBank: pages 7, 64, 65, 119; Jeroen Snijders: pages 8,
9, 15, 21, 26, 27, 29, 32, 36, 37, 38, 39, 41, 50, 51, 53, 69, 71,
74, 76, 78, 79, 82, 85, 92, 94, 97, 102, 103, 104, 105; Travel
Pictures Ltd: cover, pages 25, 30, 49, 62, 66, 87, 90, 96, 98,
99, 111, 117.

Keep us current
Information in travel guides is apt to change, which is why
we regularly update our guides. We'd be grateful to receive
feedback if you've noted something we should include in
our updates. If you have new information, please share
it with us by writing to the Commissioning Editor at the
MapStudio address on this page. The most significant
contribution to each new edition will receive a free copy of
the updated guide.

Front Cover: *Stilt fishermen at Weligama.*
Title Page: *Tea pickers, Nuwara Eliya.*

CONTENTS

1
Introducing
Sri Lanka

S ri Lanka's enduring appeal for the visitor stems from a seductive combination of tropical sunshine and superb beaches with a fascinating and colourful mosaic of cultures epitomized by the mighty relics of ancient, vanished empires. It is a combination that has allowed this teardrop-shaped island, just off the southern tip of the Indian subcontinent, to remain an attractive holiday destination despite a turbulent and tragic recent history.

Although it has close links with some of India's oldest cultures (and shares its colonial history of European occupation), it would be a mistake to think of it as an India in miniature. Sri Lanka is an island of many names, a legacy of millennia of contact with Europe, the Mediterranean and the Muslim world. To the ancient Greeks, it was Taprobane; to the Arabs, Serendib; to later European conquerors, Ceilao, Zeylan or Ceylon; and in the Sinhala tongue of most of its own people, Sri Lanka – 'Lanka the Blessed'.

Less than 50km (31 miles) from India at its closest, Sri Lanka is just 435km (270 miles) long and 225km (140 miles) across at its widest, making it easy to experience all its delights in quite a short time.

It's possible, in a fortnight, to visit the heritage sites of Anuradhapura, Sigiriya and Polonnaruwa (the island's **'cultural triangle'**), explore the tropical forests of some of the country's national parks, spend two or three days diving and snorkelling, and still have plenty of time left for lazy days on the beach, visiting lush spice gardens, shopping and sampling Sri Lanka's unique, spicy cuisine. Parts of the island

TOP ATTRACTIONS

*** **Kandy:** ancient hill capital with awesome Temple of the Buddha's Tooth.
*** **Anuradhapura:** ruined capital of Sri Lanka's greatest kingdom; being restored.
*** **Polonnaruwa:** fantastic 1000-year-old ruined city.
*** **Sigiriya:** cliff-top citadel with superb views and 1700-year-old rock paintings.
*** **Ruhuna (Yala):** elephants, leopard and rich bird life in huge national park.
** **Galle:** evocative remnants of Dutch colonial period within massive fortress walls.

◄ *Opposite: Sigiriya is one of the most striking sights in Sri Lanka.*

INTRODUCING SRI LANKA

▶ *Opposite: The ruined city of Polonnaruwa.*
▼ *Below: Sri Lanka's hill country repelled intruders until the 19th century.*

were virtually off limits during the three decades of civil strife which finally ended in 2010. Travel to the far north can still be problematic, but stretches of the beautiful east coast and several spectacular national parks which have remained almost unvisited since the 1970s are once again opening up to visitors, making Sri Lanka an even more enchanting destination.

THE LAND

Sri Lanka lies between 5 degrees 55 and 9 degrees 50 north of the Equator and south and east of India, separated from it by the Gulf of Mannar, Palk Bay and Palk Strait, which at its narrowest point, between the Indian mainland and the Jaffna Peninsula, is less than 80km (50 miles) wide. The sea crossing between Rameswaram, in India, and Mannar Island, off the northwest coast of Sri Lanka, is only around 32km (20 miles); there is no ferry or boat service.

There is evidence of a natural land bridge connecting Sri Lanka with India at this point, and indeed this vanished causeway, only a few metres below sea level, is still known as **Adam's Bridge**. This close proximity to the subcontinent has meant that Sri Lanka's history and ecology have always been exposed to strong influences from its larger neighbour.

Gemstones, Citadels and Rivers

Geologically, Sri Lanka is composed of gneiss, schist, granite, quartzite and crystalline limestone – an agglomeration that generated **rich gemstone deposits**, washed by streams and rivers from the central highlands into lowland valleys. For more than 2000 years Sri Lanka has been a noted producer

of rubies, sapphires, and semiprecious stones such as amethyst, alexandrite and topaz.

From a coastal plain, the island rises to an area of south-central highlands, which reach their highest point at **Pidurutalagala** (2524m/8281ft). As European conquerors – first the Portuguese, followed by the Dutch and finally the British – tightened their grip on the island, this hard-to-reach hill country became the final fastness of Sri Lanka's last independent rulers, the kings of Kandy. In even earlier times, they provided a refuge for island kingdoms assaulted by invaders from southern India, and as a result the hill country has an impressive concentration of once-mighty city buildings, fortresses and temples in the country.

Two major rivers flow out of the highlands – the **Mahaweli**, which flows northeast to reach the Indian Ocean near Trincomalee, and the **Walawe**, which joins the ocean near Hambantota on the south coast. A third, the **Aruvi**, flows out of the northern fringes of the highlands and the dry zone which surrounds them, emptying into Palk Bay on the north-west coast.

Harbours and Beaches

Sri Lanka's natural harbours have made the island a magnet for mariners throughout its history, from the legendary **Sindbad the Sailor** to the Portuguese navigator **Vasco da Gama** and the others who followed in search of the untold wealth of the fabled Orient. Modern visitors are as likely to be drawn by some 1600km (994 miles) of sandy beaches, warm Indian Ocean waters and coral reefs.

26 DECEMBER 2004

At 07:58 on 26 December 2004 a magnitude-9 earthquake under the ocean just west of Sumatra produced a tsunami (tidal wave) that proved to be the most devastating natural disaster in living memory. Solid walls of water surged towards the unsuspecting communities on the shores of the Indian Ocean. Sri Lanka was hit at 09:15 (local time) resulting in the loss of over 30,000 lives; almost half a million people lost their homes and all semblance of normality – roads, railways, schools and businesses – along much of the coastline were destroyed in minutes. In the aftermath of the tragedy there were fears that the country would collapse, but the capital and its vital port was undamaged and, with textiles and tea being little affected, the economy withstood the shock. Early assessments on the environment showed some sections of coastline had been badly affected, but there was minimal wave damage to many coral reefs, mangrove and dune environments. Even as early as February 2005 when scientists began their first damage reports, swathes of the landscape were showing the first signs of recovery. The human cost has been incalculable but millions of dollars have been pumped into Sri Lanka's infrastructure including a massive investment in the hotel and hospitality industries, which will lure the tourist dollar and help rebuild peoples lives.

INTRODUCING SRI LANKA

Colombo, the capital, lies on the west coast and is home to some one million of Sri Lanka's approximately 21.5 million population. Relatively few Sri Lankans are city-dwellers; of the country's other cities, none approach even Colombo's modest size. The most popular beach resorts are those closest to the capital: **Negombo**, only 35km (22 miles) north and close to the international airport, is a thriving resort and residential community of some 140,000 people. About 55–65km (30–40 miles) south of the capital, **Beruwala** and **Bentota** have merged into the island's biggest resort area, with international-standard resort hotels, restaurants and water sports, and form the gateway to a 130km (80-mile) stretch of beaches which display varying degrees of tourism development, with **Hikkaduwa**, 100km (62.5 miles) south of Colombo, forming a second resort hub. Close to the southern end of this tourism ribbon, and on the southwest corner of the island, **Galle**, with a population of 97,000, is the most important town in southern Sri Lanka. The hitherto undeveloped south coast is now a focus for major development, with Chinese investment financing a huge new seaport and an international airport at Hambantota.

▲ Above: Sun-seekers are drawn to the beaches of Sri Lanka's southwest, such as Hikkaduwa, one of the island's most popular holiday resort areas.
▶ Opposite: The rainforests around Kandy in the central hill country region shelter hundreds of birds.

COMPARATIVE CLIMATE CHART	COLOMBO				EAST COAST				KANDY			
	WIN	SPR	SUM	AUT	WIN	SPR	SUM	AUT	WIN	SPR	SUM	AUT
	JAN	APR	JULY	OCT	JAN	APR	JULY	OCT	JAN	APR	JULY	OCT
MIN TEMP. °C	22	24	25	24	24	26	26	24	8	9	13	11
MAX TEMP. °C	30	31	29	29	27	32	33	31	19	22	18	20
MIN TEMP. °F	72	75	77	75	75	78	78	75	47	49	55	52
MAX TEMP. °F	86	88	85	85	80	89	92	88	67	71	65	68
RAINFALL mm	89	231	135	348	173	58	51	221	170	119	300	269
RAINFALL in	3.5	9.1	5.3	13.7	6.8	2.3	2.0	8.7	6.7	4.7	11.8	10.6
DAYS OF RAINFALL	7	14	12	19	10	5	3	13	13	15	25	22

Climate

Only 640km (500 miles) north of the equator, Sri Lanka's **tropical** climate shows little seasonal variation in temperature. Around the coasts, temperatures hover between 26°C (78°F) and 28°C (82°F), with a mean temperature in the capital of 27.5°C (81.5°F). Inland, however, average temperatures are very much cooler. From May to September, the **southwest monsoon** deposits heavy rain on the south and west coasts, from Colombo to Galle and points east, and also raises heavy seas which make swimming and diving unattractive.

The worst intensity of the monsoon generally passes by late July or early August. The north and east, including the main east coast port of Trincomalee, are affected by the **northeast monsoon** betwen November and February, but this will have little impact on most visitors, as the main resort areas and visitor attractions are concentrated in the south and the central hills. Local thunderstorms can occur at any time of year, and while these are often intense they do not usually last more than a few hours.

Fauna

Encompassing habitats which range from dry zone scrub, mangrove swamp, and lowland rain forest to cloud forest and cultivated land, Sri Lanka is among Asia's most **biologically diverse** countries.

National Parks

Kankesanturai   Point Pedro
Jaffna
                        Chundikkulam
                        Bird Sanctuary
Kilinochchi

INDIAN
OCEAN

Mullaittivu

0   20 km
0   10 miles

Madhu Road
Sanctuary
Mannar   Kokkilai Bird
                      Sanctuary

Giant's Tank
Sanctuary
                    Vavuniya

                Naval Headworks
                Sanctuary   Trincomalee

Wilpattu
National Park   Anuradhapura   Mutur
                        Somawathie
                        Chaitiya Sanctuary
            Ritigala Strict
            Nature Reserve   Trikonamadu
Puttalam   Nature Reserve
            Minneriya
            Giritale Sanctuary Polonnaruwa

            Wasgomuwa Strict
            Nature Reserve
Chilaw   Batticaloa
                        Madura Oya
                        National Park
Kurunegala   Matale

            Kandy
Negombo   Kegalla   Victoria Randenigala   Ampara
                    Rantambe Sanctuary
        Gampaha   Gal Oya
                    Galways Land   National Park
COLOMBO   National Park
            Nuwara Eliya   Badulla
Panadura   Peak Wilderness Horton   Lahugala
            Sanctuary   Plains NP National Park Pottuvil
        Ratnapura
                    Uda Walawe   Yala East
Beruwala   National Park Ruhuna (Yala) National Park
                            National Park Kumana
Bentota   Sinharaja   Ruhuna Wildlife
        Biosphere Reserve Wirawila Tissa Wildlife Sanctuary
                    Bird Sanctuary Sanctuary
                Hambantota Bundala
        Galle Weligama   National Park
                    Tangalla
                Matara

N

INTRODUCING SRI LANKA

▼ *Below: The Sri Lankan frogmouth, a relative of the nightjar, is endemic to the island.*

Sri Lanka is rich in wildlife, which has at least partly been protected by the Buddhist taboo on the taking of life. This provides little protection, however, against habitat destruction, and the country's many national parks and wildlife reserves probably play a more important part in ensuring the survival of endemic bird and animal species. Among the most exciting and accessible of the national parks is **Ruhuna (Yala)**, 309km (190 miles) southeast of Colombo and covering some 1259km² (486 sq miles) of open plains, dense jungle, and Indian Ocean shoreline. Large numbers of wild elephants may still be found here.

Orphaned young elephants whose parents have been the victims of poachers or accidents are cared for at the **Elephant Orphanage**, off the Colombo–Kandy main road. Other large mammal species include wild buffalo, whose domesticated relatives can often be seen ploughing or pulling carts; five deer species, including sambur, spotted deer, hog deer and mouse deer; and the island's only bear species, the elusive sloth bear, found in lowland forests. Monkeys include the red macaque, grey langur, leaf monkey and bear monkey, as well as the slow-moving nocturnal loris; and the squirrel family includes the small palm squirrel, flying squirrel, and giant squirrel. Reptiles include two types of crocodile, the river crocodile and marsh crocodile; several species of monitor, gecko and chameleon; and more than 90 snake species, among them the cobra, which often appears in Buddhist and Hindu mythology.

Offshore, Sri Lanka is ringed by a **wide coral shelf**. While this has not escaped the degradation that has affected coral reefs worldwide, it still provides superb diving, sheltering fish species including emperor angel, moorish idol, powder-blue surgeon, sergeant-major, lion fish, unicorn fish, and a variety of parrot fish species. Pelagic species and game fish include marlin, pompano, ranax, yellowfin and barracuda, jack, and dog-tooth tuna. Sea mammals sighted off the south coast can include Sperm whales, Bryde's whales, Spinner dolphins and Blue whales which are regularly seen in December and April.

Plant Life

As with its fauna, Sri Lanka's wide **range of habitats** provides niches for a bewildering array of plant species, from shoreline plants like mangrove to rainforest giants, succulents and thorn trees adapted to live in the dry zone, and tiny high-altitude species capable of finding a place among rocky peaks and bare boulders. Sri Lanka is still well forested, with more than 8000ha (19,768 acres) of virgin, uninhabited woodland in the Sinharaja Forest alone. Sinharaja is reputed to shelter some 120 tree species, including ironwood, satinwood, teak, ebony and flamboyant. The **'bo-'** or **'bodhi tree'** (*Ficus religiosa*), a species of fig, is sacred to the Lord Buddha and is found throughout the island. Rhododendron forests grow on the hillsides of the Horton Plains region. Cultivated trees include coconut palm, which yields oil, copra, desiccated coconut, and alcoholic 'arrack'. Rubber, introduced by the British as a cash crop, is grown below the 600m (1969ft) contour.

Numerous **spices** grow here, including cinnamon, pepper, cardamom, cloves and nutmeg – these were among the treasures which first drew Arab and European traders to Sri Lanka. Visitors will find a delicious array of fresh fruit, from familiar varieties such as banana, papaya, pineapple, mango and guava to local seasonal varieties such as mangosteen, rambutan and the strong-smelling durian.

But perhaps the plant for which Sri Lanka is most famous is tea, which flourishes in the high country, growing well between 600m (1969ft) and 1800m (5906ft) above sea level. Tea from Sri Lanka – still mostly marketed under the name of **'Ceylon' tea** – is reckoned among the world's finest and a visit to a tea plantation is part of most sightseeing tours of the island.

MARINE TURTLES

Five species of marine turtle nest on Sri Lanka's beaches. All are **threatened** by loss of habitat due to encroaching tourism development and by the slaughter of adult turtles for meat and shell.

At Rekewa, 200km (124 miles) south of Colombo, the Turtle Conservation project set up in the late 1990s protects a 2km (1.2-mile) stretch of beach where all five species – loggerhead, leatherback, Olive Ridley, green and hawksbill – lay their eggs. In the aftermath of the tsunami, Rekewa and another turtle nesting beach at Bundala have been named as sea turtle sanctuaries, the first such protected areas on the island.

INTRODUCING SRI LANKA

HISTORY IN BRIEF
Early History

The earliest traces of human habitation in Sri Lanka date from the **Old Stone Age** of about 1,750,000 years ago, and archaeological evidence suggests that later hunter-gatherers wandered across a land bridge between the Indian subcontinent and Sri Lanka some 10,000 years ago. In the ancient Hindu epic, the *Ramayana*, Lanka (not yet blessed with the prefix 'Sri') appears as the homeland of the demon king Ravana, who kidnaps Sita, wife of the hero Rama.

THE MAHAVANSA

The Mahavansa, the **genealogical chronicle** of the kings of Lanka, was rediscovered in the last century by a Ceylon-born Englishman, **George Turnour** (1799–1843). Aided by a well-read Buddhist monk, Turnour found a prose *tika* or explanation of the Mahavansa in a palm-leaf manuscript and with the help of this translated and edited the epic saga – an unbroken record of more than 2400 years of history and the reigns of 164 kings. The Mahavansa is among the most important sources for historians studying the country's past. Beginning with the arrival of King Vijaya and his followers, it was first written down by Buddhist monks in AD 500 and ends only with the decline of the last Kandyan kingdom.

The Maurya Empire

The earliest historical record is the remarkable account of the arrival of the **Prince Vijaya** from southern India some-time in the 5th century BC. His arrival is chronicled in the Mahavansa, and relates how Prince Vijaya, having been expelled by his father, landed and conquered the three indigenous tribes. This account forms the basis of Sinhalese tradition and understanding of the Sinhalese people's roots in the island. The Sinhalese language has features in common with those of northern India, whilst the language of the Tamils, the other major ethnic group in Sri Lanka, is related closely to the Dravidian languages of southern India. This ethnic difference has created a divide amongst the peoples of Sri Lanka which continues to cause major problems to this day. Firmer historical data begins to appear around the 3rd century BC, when the Maurya Empire of India embraced Sri Lanka, bringing with it the Buddhist faith that remains a distinguishing feature of the nation's culture some 2300 years on. It was during the Mauryan era, too, that Europe first heard of Sri Lanka, when rumour of a land rich in gems and spices reached the ears of Megasthenes, Alexander the Great's envoy to the Mauryan court.

A Golden Age

Sinhalese tradition states that the third king of the Vijaya dynasty, **Pandukhabhaya**, founded the city of Anuradhapura which was to be the seat of government for over a thousand years. The remains of this remarkable city were rediscovered by the British in the 19th century, and comprise the evidence of the scale and complexity of the early civilizations that existed in Asia. This is the city where, according to Buddhist legend, a sapling of the bo-tree under which the Buddha achieved enlightenment was planted. Anuradhapura was eventually abandoned as the capital in the 11th century as a result of its northern location, which made it vulnerable to frequent raids and invasions from southern India. King Vijayabahu I chose Polonnaruwa, further to the southeast, as his new capital precisely because it was further away from India and less vulnerable to attack.

Both Anuradhapura and Polonnaruwa relied on a sophisticated artificial irrigation system of canals and large man-made reservoirs or 'tanks'. Constant feuding and even foreign adventures such as that of King Parakramabahu I (1153–86), who attacked Burma, led to the decay of the irrigation system and eventually to the abandonment of Polonnaruwa. There then followed a prolonged period of confusion, as rival Sinhalese rulers fought each other and various intruders. These internal conflicts made the island easy prey for invaders. In 1247 and again in 1258 the island was raided by Malay pirate sultans, and in 1411 the Chinese admiral Chen Ho abducted a local king. Internal divisions and factional dynastic quarrels meant that by the early 16th century the island was divided into three kingdoms: a Tamil kingdom in the north, with the Sinhalese kingdoms of Kandy in the centre and Kotte in the south and along the coastline. Then in 1505 a storm blew into Colombo a Portuguese fleet.

ADVENT OF BUDDHISM

Buddhism arrived in Sri Lanka in the 2nd century BC, and is the **religion** followed by the majority of the **Sinhalese** population. The Tamils in the north and east of the country are Hindus, as are the Tamils of southern India, with whom the Tamils of Sri Lanka have a close cultural affinity. Buddhism as a religion was largely forced out of India by resurgent Hinduism in the 3rd century BC, but survived in Lanka, which today is one of a handful of countries – including Burma, Cambodia, Thailand and Tibet – where it is the majority faith.

◄ *Opposite: Relics of the Anuradhapura period, like this female statue, can be seen in the National Archaeological Museum in Colombo.*

INTRODUCING SRI LANKA

The Portuguese

Portugal in the late 15th and early 16th centuries was an aggressively expanding power. **Vasco da Gama** had rounded the Cape of Good Hope in 1498 and reached India. The fleet that came to Sri Lanka in 1505 was a follow-up to that voyage. What the Portuguese were seeking was access to the spices of the east.

The Portuguese tapped into the sophisticated trade networks that existed, and became inextricably involved in local politics and power struggles. They first traded with, then assisted the Kings of Kotte in their struggles with their neighbours, and then ended up controlling Kotte. The most profitable trade was in spice, mainly in the form of cinnamon, and later ginger, nutmeg and pepper.

The Portuguese also came with a mission to spread the Roman Catholic faith. Religion could also be used as a means of control, and the Portuguese success in converting Prince Dharmapala in 1557 meant that he was little more than a Portuguese puppet. By an agreement in 1543 the Portuguese were confirmed in their control of Kotte and the coast, and guaranteed the defence of Sri Lanka in return for a tribute of cinnamon, but they never controlled the interior of the island, and their control of the coast ended in 1658 when they were ousted by the Dutch.

The Dutch

The foundation in 1600 of the Dutch East India Company, or VOC, had been designed to wrest control of far eastern markets from the hands of the Dutch Republic's enemies, Spain and Portugal. The Dutch enlisted local allies, in particular the Kingdom of Kandy, but like the Portuguese they never controlled the whole of the island. Kandy, in the inaccessible, mountainous and heavily forested interior, was able to maintain its independence. Like the Portuguese the Dutch were attracted by the spice trade, and the island was also an important staging point on the VOC's trade routes to the East Indies, China and Japan. When the Dutch Republic declined at the end of the 18th century, its possessions

overseas became natural targets for Britain, which seized the island in 1796, renaming it **Ceylon**.

▲ Above: The gates and walls which surround the port of Galle date from the Dutch colonial era.

British Rule

The Congress of Vienna (1815) confirmed the British in possession of Sri Lanka, and they turned their attention to conquering Kandy. They built military roads to make the inland kingdom accessible, and Kandy was quickly conquered, ending more than 2000 years of independence. A revolt in 1818 was suppressed with great severity, burning fields and villages, and some districts took decades to recover. As in India, the British set out to change the nature of the country over which they were ruling.

In 1833 a series of reforms introduced an element of Sinhalese participation in the government, with the aim of regenerating Sri Lankan society along European lines. The main thrust though was economic liberation, which was followed by the introduction of coffee-growing on large plantations. To work these large plantations labour was required, and the Sinhalese were unwilling to work for the low wages offered. The solution was the importation of Indian

THE CHINESE

In 1405, the great Chinese navigator **Chen Ho** arrived in Sri Lanka on a voyage that ultimately took him as far as Africa. Foolishly, the Sinhalese ruler Vijayabahu IV tried to kidnap Chen Ho. He failed, and paid the price six years later when the Chinese returned in force, captured the king and took him in chains to Peking. The Chinese made one of his rivals, Sri Parakrama Bahu VI, king in his place. From 1434–48 Sri Lanka paid tribute to China, but by the end of the 15th century the Chinese had lost interest in their overseas possession and the link was broken.

▲ *Above: Sri Lanka's highlands produce some of the world's finest teas, which are picked by hand.*

COFFEE

The British introduced coffee-growing to Sri Lanka in 1824, hoping for a more lucrative crop to replace cinnamon. By the 1840s coffee was king, with hundreds of thousands of acres of forest in the Kandyan highlands cleared to make way for plantations. But in 1869 disaster struck in the shape of 'coffee rust' (*Hemileia vastratrix*) which over the next 20 years laid the plantations to waste. Many of the European planters and Sinhalese involved in coffee-growing were ruined.

Tamils, ethnically related to the Tamils already present in Sri Lanka, but from southern India. This immigration was to cause problems later, especially in the post-independence period. Coffee failed as a crop in the 1870s due to a leaf blight, and production was switched to tea.

Rubber was also an imported product that was cultivated on the island, and started by the British. Few Britons actually settled in Sri Lanka, and when nationalist stirrings did start, it was not possible for Britain to retain control indefinitely.

The British response to riots and disturbances in 1915 was repression, followed by concessions to nationalist demands. In 1919 the creation of the **Ceylon National Congress** united previous Sinhalese and Tamil organizations agitating for greater involvement in government. Pressure for change came mainly from those who had received a western education, but who also felt threatened on religious and cultural grounds by the British domination of the country. A new constitution which took account of those demands was implemented in 1920, and then amended in 1924. That response was developed in 1931 with further constitutional changes which created a universal franchise and the inclusion of Sinhalese and Tamils in government. There was little opposition to the British during WWII, and the nationalist cause was rewarded by the 1945 Soulbury Commission which drew up a constitution based on the Westminster model, and would confer independence. Elections were held at the end of 1947, and the country was **granted independence** on **4 February 1948**.

Post-Independence

The **United National Party** (UNP), which won the elections of 1947, was dominated by the western-educated elite. Seen as unresponsive to the needs of most Sri Lankans, the UNP was ousted in 1956 elections by the **Sri Lankan Freedom Party**, a nationalist-leftist group which pandered to Sinhalese chauvinism, making Sinhala the sole official language. This angered the Tamil community, setting the scene for the troubles that bedevilled the country for the next decades. Ceylon was renamed Sri Lanka under a new constitution in 1972, and Buddhism was reinforced as the country's foremost religion. In 1977, the UNP returned to power and changed the constitution again, creating a system headed by an executive president. Junius Richard Jayewardene was the first leader to be elected to this office.

Open violence between Tamil and Sinhalese communities broke out with anti-Tamil riots in 1983, followed by armed Tamil resistance spearheaded by the **Liberation Tigers of Tamil Eelam**

▼ *Below: The milky sap of the rubber tree is still an important foreign currency earner.*

INTRODUCING SRI LANKA

(LTTE), which called for an independent Tamil state in the north, where most of Sri Lanka's Tamil people live. In 1987, an **Indian Peace Keeping Force** was deployed in the north, but failed in its task and was withdrawn in 1990, when the Sri Lankan military took over the anti-insurgency task.

The conflict continued for the next 20 years, varying in intensity. In 1993, President Ranasinghe Premadasa was assassinated, allegedly by a Tamil extremist. In 2000, the LTTE attempted to assassinate President Chandra Kumaratunga, and although a ceasefire was negotiated in 2002 neither the LTTE nor the government seemed sincerely committed to the peace process, with the LTTE withdrawing from talks in 2003 and one of its factions renewing violence in 2004. In January 2008 the government launched a full-scale military offensive against the LTTE's northern strongholds. In 2009, the army overran the last rebel-held areas, LTTE leader Velupillai Prabhakaran was killed, and the government declared complete victory. This was, however, accomplished only with heavy civilian casualties. Over almost 30 years, the war was estimated to have cost more than 100,000 lives.

The government was criticised too for interning hundreds of thousands of Tamil civilians, who were only gradually released in 2009–10.

Mahinda Rajapaksa, elected president in 2005 and re-elected in 2010, sought a third term in 2015 but lost out to **Maithripala Sirisena**, a former ally, a result which surprised many. Sirisena won 51.2% of the vote on an 81% turnout,

attracting substantial support from Tamil and Muslim voters, and formed an unwieldy coalition government of ethnic, religious, Marxist and centre-right parties. His success was due mainly to resentment of the Rajapaksa clan's perceived nepotism. Three of the Former president's brothers had been appointed to senior government roles, and Rajapakasa was widely seen to be grooming his son Namal (elected MP for Hambantota in 2010) as his successor. Sirisena, leader of the centre-right Sri Lanka Freedom Party and a career politician since 1989, gave no sign that he would depart from Rajapaksa's economic policies or yield to calls for investigation into alleged war crimes.

◀ *Opposite: Muslims and Hindus are represented by green and saffron stripes on the flag. There are bo-leaves in each corner.*

HISTORICAL CALENDAR

1,750,000 years ago Earliest artefacts found, described as Old Stone Age or Palaeolithic.

5000 years ago New Stone Age marks transformation to a settled way of life.

5th Century BC According to Sinhalese legend the arrival of Prince Vijaya at Puttolom; arrival of the first Aryan-Indian settlers from India.

2nd Century BC Arrival of Buddhism.

AD65 Fall of Vijaya dynasty, and takeover by Lambakannas rulers who controlled the island for four centuries.

1283 King Bhuvanaika Buhu I sends an emissary to the Sultan of Egypt.

14th Century Division of the island into Sinhalese kingdoms in south and centre, and Tamil kingdoms in north and east.

1505 The Portuguese arrive.

1543 Treaty between King Bhuvanaika Bahu and Portugal, confirming Portuguese possessions and privileges.

1658 Dutch seize control of the island from Portugal.

1796 Britain ousts the Dutch.

1815 Fall of Kandyan kingdom.

1919 Formation of Ceylon National Congress.

1920 Granting of new constitution by British. Modified in 1924 to take account of nationalist aspirations.

1931 Constitution changed to allow creation of a State Council, a universal franchise, and an element of Ceylonese participation in government.

1945 Soulbury Commission drafts constitution for the independent state of Ceylon.

1948, 4 February Independence from Britain as Commonwealth member.

1947 Elections won by United National Party (UNP), led by Don Stephen Senanayake, who became the first prime minister of Ceylon.

1956 Defeat of UNP. Sri Lanka Freedom Party (SLFP) promotes a version of nationalism allied with socialism; led by S W R D Bandaranaike.

1959 Assassination of Bandaranaike; his wife Sirimavo became prime minister in 1960.

1965 Re-election of UNP led by son of first prime minister, Dudley Shelton Senanayake, in response to the instability of the SLFP administration.

1970 Return of the SLFP and Sirimara Bandaranaike as prime minister.

1972 Change of country's name from Ceylon to present-day Republic of Sri Lanka.

1972 New constitution; Sinhala is official language.

1977 SLFP defeated; UNP takes office under Junius Richard Jayewardene. Constitution changes to one based on French model with executive president.

1983 Series of anti-Tamil riots especially in Colombo.

1987 Governments of Sri Lanka and India put an Indian Peace Keeping Force (IPKF) in the north. Tamil separatists, especially Liberation Tigers of Tamil Eelam (LTTE), fall out with India; fighting resumes.

1989 Jayewardene retires and is succeeded by Ranasinghe Premadasa.

1990 Negotiated withdrawal of the IPKF, Sri Lankan military take over.

1993 Assassination of Ranasinghe Premadasa, allegedly by a Tamil extremist.

2004 Tsunami causes heavy damage and kills some 30,000 people.

2005 Mahinda Rajapaksa is elected President.

2008 Army launches final offensive against LTTE.

2008 Arugam Bay Bridge, destroyed by tsunami, re-opens.

2009 Government announces the complete defeat of LTTE.

2015 Rajapaksa loses presidential election to Maithripala Sirisena.

2015 Pope Francis visits Sri Lanka.

INTRODUCING SRI LANKA

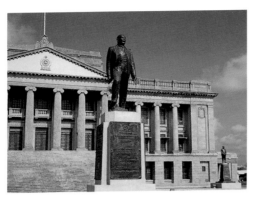

GOVERNMENT AND ECONOMY

Sri Lanka declared itself a republic in 1972, but opted to stay within the **British Commonwealth**, maintaining close links with Britain and other Commonwealth countries. The president is head of state and executive chief of government, and appoints the cabinet. The prime minister's role is mainly ceremonial. Both are elected for a six-year term, as are the 225 members of the single-chamber parliament. The next elections are due in 2016. In the 2010 elections, the United People's Freedom Alliance emerged as the largest party, with just under 61 per cent of the vote and 144 parliamentary seats, followed by the United National Party with just under 30 per cent and 60 seats. Smaller parties in parliament include the Democratic National Alliance and the Tamil National Alliance.

Economic Development

Since independence, the government has aimed to diversify and modernize the economy, which under British rule depended on exporting tea, rubber and coconut products. These and other commodities remain important, but since the early 1980s governments have liberalized the economy to attract international investment and encourage the private sector.

China has become one of the country's most important business partners, with two Chinese companies investing upwards of US$1 billion to create South Asia's largest seaport on the south coast at Hambantota. Along with a new international airport and a large freeport zone which opened in 2010, this is expected to provide jobs for more than 50,000 people.

Before the tsunami of 2004, Sri Lanka's economy was experiencing buoyant growth, and huge amounts of foreign

THE BANDARANAIKE FAMILY

In 1925, Solomon West Ridgeway Dias Bandaranaike, Oxford-educated son of a wealthy Christian landowner, rejected his father's Christian and pro-British sympathies to form the Sinhalese Popular Congress, which later merged into the United National Party. Deserting the UNP in 1951, he formed the Sri Lanka Freedom Party. The party's pro-Sinhalese Buddhist, anti-Tamil sectarianism swept it to power in 1956. S W R D Bandaranaike was assassinated by a Buddhist monk in 1959. His widow, Sirimavo Bandaranaike, took over the Freedom Party and was in and out of power through the 1960s and 1970s. She was ousted in 1977, but in 1994 her daughter, Chandrika Bandaranaike Kumaratunga, became leader of the party and was elected as the country's first female president. She appointed her mother as prime minister.

aid were pumped into the country to aid recovery after the disaster, with the USA contributing more than US$134.5 million to rebuild infrastructure, rebuild schools and create sustainable jobs.

The Development Credit Guarantee programme, a partnership between USAID and the Lanka Orix Leasing company, provides up to US$5 million in micro-loans to help farmers and small enterprises in eastern Sri Lanka, the region hardest hit by the tsunami.

The impact of the worldwide recession was alleviated by an IMF provisional bailout of US$2.6 billion in 2009, and although growth slowed briefly, the economy continued to expand by an estimated 6.9 per cent in 2010. The end of the civil war is likely to give the economy a further boost. During the conflict, military spending accounted for almost 20 per cent of the national budget, and the advent of peace may free some of this expenditure for more peaceful uses.

TEA

The first tea was planted in Sri Lanka at the **Royal Botanical Gardens** in Peradeniya in 1824, but tea-growing did not become important until the late 1860s, when it was given impetus by the failure of the coffee crop. By the end of the 19th century, the island was exporting almost 68 million kilograms (150 million pounds) of tea annually. Today, about 202,000ha (500,000 acres) of land in the hill areas are devoted to growing tea, and Sri Lanka is the world's largest exporter of what is recognized as some of the world's finest tea.

Trade and Industry

A well-educated workforce (with a national literacy rate more than 90 per cent), coupled with low wages and incentives such as tax-free Export Processing Zones (EPZs), have made textiles and garment-making into Sri Lanka's largest foreign currency earner, accounting for almost 50 per cent of export earnings. Remittances from Sri Lankans working overseas (mainly in the Middle East and the EU) are also a significant source of foreign currency.

Tea, which was once central to the economy, now accounts for only 15 per cent of exports, and while agriculture still employs one in three Sri Lankan workers it accounts for only 12.6 per cent of GDP. By contrast, the service sector employs 57.6 per cent of the workforce and industry provides 30 per cent of jobs.

◀ *Opposite: The Presidential Secretariat, the former Parliament of Sri Lanka.*
▼ *Below: Three-wheelers like this one are the cheapest way of getting around Colombo.*

INTRODUCING SRI LANKA

Despite growth and modernization, Sri Lanka remains very much a developing economy, and 23 per cent of Sri Lankans are estimated to live below the poverty line. People trafficking, including the trafficking of children for sexual purposes, is an issue, and despite new legislation making it easier to prosecute traffickers and visitors who abuse children, there have been few if any arrests, prosecutions or convictions of such offenders.

Tourism has been surprisingly successful despite the country's troubles, and the tourism industry is worth some US$0.36 billion (SL Rupees 40 billion) annually, with 1.3 million people visiting Sri Lanka in 2010. Tourism's prospects look rosy: according to official statistics, the number of visitors in 2014 was up by 27 per cent compared with the previous year.

THE PEOPLE

Sri Lanka's population in 2010 was estimated at 21,513,990. Population growth slowed somewhat during the first decade of the 21st century (from 1.14 per cent in 2001 to 0.863 per cent in 2008). Population density, at just under 300 people per square kilometre, is relatively high. Only around 15 per cent of Sri Lankans live in large towns and cities, with the population of the capital, Colombo and the surrounding metropolitan area, estimated at around 2,000,000. Only a handful of other cities, including Kandy, the resort areas of Negombo and Beruwala, and the 'gem city' of Ratnapura, have populations of more than 100,000, although Hambantota, with its new seaport and airport, is growing rapidly into a major urban centre.

Ethnic Mix

Around 72 per cent of Sri Lankans are ethnic Sinhalese, who in turn tend to divide themselves into 'low country' dwellers in the coastal towns and lowlands, and 'Kandyan' inhabitants of the hill country. Many Kandyans are said by lowlanders to consider themselves a cut above their coastal cousins, as descendants of the Kandyans who were the last Sri Lankans

to fall under the sway of a European colonial power.

Around 13 per cent of the population are Sri Lankan Tamils. Descendants of south Indian migrants who began to arrive in Sri Lanka as long as 2000 years ago, crossing the narrow Palk Strait between Sri Lanka and what is now the Indian state of Tamil Nadu, their heartland is in the north and east of the country, around Jaffna in the extreme north, the port of Trincomalee, and Batticaloa on the east coast. The civil war which lasted until 2009 claimed up to 100,000 lives and drove up to 700,000 people from their homes. Some 200,000 Tamils are estimated to have emigrated during the conflict, to the UK and other European Union countries, Canada, Australia, the USA and India. Many Tamils remain in exile.

A further 6 per cent of the population are 'Indian' Tamils, descendants of labourers imported by the British to work in the tea plantations of the hill country in the 19th century – employment which the proud Kandyans of the region, still smarting from their conquest by Britain, refused to consider. Though they have been the victims in the past of language

THE BURGHERS

Sri Lanka's tiny Burgher community, descended from Dutch and Portuguese colonialists, played a major part in running the country under British rule, when they formed an educated, English-speaking class which dominated the administration and the professions. After independence, however, their position was eroded as successive governments promoted Sinhalese as the national language, and Burghers were treated with some suspicion. Many have emigrated to the UK and to Australia, and there are now probably fewer than 15,000 people of Burgher descent in Sri Lanka.

discrimination and outbursts of ethnic violence, the hill-country Tamils have mainly stayed uninvolved with the conflict in the north and east.

Sri Lankans of Arab descent, locally known as 'Moors' – though their ancestors may have arrived from the Gulf states as much as 1000 years ago – and 'Malays', descended from workers imported from the East Indies by the Dutch and the British, account for around 8 per cent of the population, and the 'Burgher' community, the Christian descendants of Portuguese and Dutch settlers who intermarried with the Sinhalese, account for a tiny minority of less than 1 per cent, most of them resident in Colombo and Galle.

Regardless of the country's colonial past and its present-day troubles, Sri Lankans of all ethnic groups are generally extremely friendly, helpful and welcoming to visitors in their country.

Language

Language has been a contentious issue in Sri Lanka. In the 1970s, Sinhalese demagogues promoted efforts to make Sinhala – the language of the Sinhalese majority – the sole language of education, administration and government. This was perceived by the Tamil minority as a deliberate move to keep Tamils out of government and exclude them from further education, and was a major cause of the discontent that eventually erupted into inter-communal violence. Subsequently, a compromise was reached in an attempt to satisfy both the disgruntled Tamil community and hard-line Sinhalese nationalists. **Tamil** and **Sinhala** are ranked equally as 'official' languages, while Sinhala is the 'national' language. Tamil – which is also the largest language group in southern India and the main language of Tamil Nadu, the Indian state closest to Sri Lanka – is the mother tongue of about 20 per cent of the population in total, including both northern and hill-country 'Indian' Tamil communities, while Sinhala is the first language of the Sinhalese majority and of most Sri Lankans of Malay and Arab descent.

WHAT'S IN A NAME?

The Sinhalese name for their island, **Sinhaladvipa** (land of the lion people) was corrupted into the Arabic '**Serendib**' by Muslim traders, then into '**Ceilao**' by the Portuguese, and from that version into '**Zeylan**' by the Dutch, before being anglicized as '**Ceylon**' by the British in the 18th century. In **1972** the island's name officially became **Sri Lanka**.

Meanwhile, **English** is still almost universally spoken by educated people of all communities, and is the language with which Sri Lanka communicates with the outside world. Despite being the language of the former colonial power, English is also politically neutral. Most of the people you are likely to encounter in shops, hotels, restaurants and when travelling on public transport are likely to speak enough English for you to get by. Taxi drivers usually speak some English, and bus and railway personnel are usually quite fluent. Out in the countryside, English may be less widely spoken, though it is rare to find yourself completely unable to communicate.

Religion

Sri Lanka's majority religion is the austere Theravada ('small vehicle') school of Buddhism, imported from India during the 3rd century bc and followed today by the vast majority of the Sinhalese ethnic group.

In 1972 **Buddhism** was made virtually a national religion, and acknowledged by the government as the country's paramount faith, a move which disturbed Tamil Hindus and members of other faiths. **Hinduism**, an even older religion, is the faith of the Tamil minority, while there are significant **Muslim** and **Christian** minorities which each account for between 7 and 8 per cent of the population. The Christian community comprises the descendants of the early Portuguese and Dutch colonists who intermarried with local communities, as well as converts from both the Sinhalese Buddhist and Tamil Hindu communities. The Muslim community also includes Sinhalese and Tamil converts, but

> ### THE EIGHT-FOLD PATH
>
> The Buddha taught that all life is suffering; that this suffering comes from selfish desire; that eliminating selfish desire from one's life is the way to escape suffering; and that the Buddhist 'eight-fold path' or 'middle way' is the way to achieve this. The 'eight rights' which make up the eight-fold path are right understanding, right thought, right speech, right action, right aspiration, right exertion, right attentiveness and right concentration.

▼ *Below: Images of the Buddha are revered by Sri Lanka's Buddhist majority and are found all over the island.*

HINDUISM

With its dozens of deities, many of whom have several different personalities, Hinduism baffles the outsider. There are three major deities: **Brahma**, the creator; **Vishnu**, the preserver; and **Shiva**, who represents destruction and rebirth. All-seeing Brahma, the most remote of the gods from humankind, is depicted with four faces, often accompanied by his consort, the goddess Sarasvati. Shiva is represented by the stone lingam, a stylized penis symbolizing virility and male fertility. Vishnu is the most human of the three great Hindu gods, appearing in a series of incarnations which symbolize the nine ages of the world. In his first six incarnations he appeared in the form of a wild boar or a manticore (half-man, half-lion), but in his seventh he appeared as King Rama, leader of mankind and the gods against Ravana, the demon-king of Lanka in Hinduism's most accessible epic, the *Ramayana*. Hinduism also has a large supporting cast of lesser deities, like Rama's faithful ally Hanuman, king of the monkeys; and Ganesha, elephant-headed son of Shiva and his consort Parvati, and god of wisdom and wealth.

its numbers are bolstered by the descendants of Arab traders from the Gulf, who arrived as early as the 7th century AD, and by people of Malay descent, whose ancestors were imported from the East Indies as labourers by the Dutch and later by the British.

There is a certain amount of overlap between faiths, with Christians and Muslims praying alongside Hindus and Buddhists at some holy places, such as Kataragama in the southeast and Adams Peak in the highlands.

Hinduism, the faith of Sri Lanka's Tamil minority, is the oldest and most complex faith in the world. Born in the Indus Valley with the Indian subcontinent's first civilization, its pantheon was added to by Aryan invaders who arrived in India from the north in around 1500BC.

Buddhism, the faith of Sri Lanka's Sinhalese majority, grew from Hinduism and retains some of the elements of

the Hindu religion, such as a belief in reincarnation. Unlike Hinduism – and uniquely among the world's great faiths – Buddhism has no gods, and in that sense is a philosophy and a code of conduct rather than a religion as such.

Buddhism began some 2500 years ago with the teachings of Siddartha Gautama, prince of a north Indian Hindu dynasty, who gave up his earthly power and wealth in achieving enlightenment.

Bhuddhism's greatest convert was the Mauryan Emperor Ashok, whose realm at its most powerful comprised almost all the subcontinent (except for the far south), and who sent his son Mahindra to carry the Buddha's teachings to the Lankan kings of Anuradhapura. There, it found an enthusiastic following, and the Sinhalese kingdoms remained firmly Buddhist long after Buddhism had waned on the Indian mainland.

Christianity was brought to Sri Lanka by the Portuguese, and the overwhelming majority of Sri Lanka's 900,000-strong Christian minority still follow the Roman Catholic faith of the first Christian converts, with only around 120,000 adhering to other Christian churches.

Sport and Recreation

Sri Lankans have triumphed internationally at **athletics**, among them, in the 1990s, the sprinter Susanthika Jayasinghe (who won a bronze medal in the 200m in the 2000 Olympic Games in Sydney) and others, including Sriyani Kulawansa and Sugath Tillekeratne. But it is **cricket** that is the first and truest love of all Sri Lankan sport fans. When Sri Lanka, led by Arjuna Ranatunga, trounced the giants of world cricket to win the 1996 World Cup in

◄ *Opposite: Hindu temples, like this one in Negombo, are brilliantly colourful and covered in statues of gods and goddesses.*
▼ *Below: Colombo's Galle Face Green is a popular spot for a game of cricket.*

▲ *Above: Kandyan dancers perform to the rhythms of wooden drums.*

one-day internationals, there was dancing in the streets, and when Sri Lanka's team is playing in major international events it is with the whole island watching or listening. Players are major stars, and probably the most popular public figures in the country. Any patch of relatively flat wasteland or village square is likely to have its complement of small boys playing an improvised game, and no matter how crude or aged the equipment, the players will be as deadly serious as any world cup final team. Cricket is played from January to April at Colombo's Kettarama Stadium and Asgiriya in Kandy, while a new stadium at Hambantota hosted two Cricket World Cup fixtures in 2011. Sri Lanka is also bidding to host the Commonwealth Games in 2018.

Sri Lanka also abounds in **water sports**, with some excellent scuba diving from qualified dive shops at major resorts, and windsurfing and sailing equipment for hire at all the re-opened beach resort areas. These, however, are sports intended primarily for visiting holiday-makers, though some Sri Lankans have taken them up too.

THE ARTS

Sri Lankan visual arts, architecture, literature, music and dance all bear the stamp of the country's centuries-old Buddhist culture. Poetry, as well as music and dance, were almost entirely ceremonial and devotional until well after the fall of the Kandyan kingdom to the British, but by the mid-19th century Sri Lanka was being opened up to outside

GRATIAEN MEMORIAL PRIZE

Michael Ondaatje's international success has enabled him to establish the Gratiaen Memorial Prize. This is for works in English by Sri Lankan authors and has been won in recent years by Carl Muller (1993), for *The Jam Fruit Tree*, first in a trilogy of works about a Colombo Burgher dynasty.

cultural influences by the advent of the printing press. However, Sri Lanka has its share of literary talent, including the prize-winning Michael Ondaatje, author of *The English Patient* and other novels.

The 43 Group of visual artists, founded in 1943, was a major force in fusing Asian and Western artistic influences, led by painters such as Harry Pieris (1904–88), Justin Daraniyagala (1903–67) and others.

Music and Dance

Music and dance in Sri Lanka are still closely tied up with religious ritual. Kandyan or 'high country' dance has evolved from village dances performed to appeal to local deities, and is accompanied by the complex rhythms of several drummers who use a percussion instrument called the *gatebere* – a wooden drum with leather heads of monkey skin at one end and cowhide at the other, which make contrasting tones.

Dancers, usually women, go through a routine of sinuous poses and flowing arm movements. 'Low country' or 'devil-mask' dancing is also accompanied by drummers, who use a special 'demon drum' to enhance the steps and movements of dancers wearing the grotesque masks which represent the 18 demons of disease. These dances were – and sometimes still are – performed with the intention of persuading the demon to leave the afflicted person.

Art and Architecture

The most prominent examples of Sri Lanka's Buddhist-influenced architectural heritage are the dagobas which can be seen from one end of the country to the other. In the

FRESCOES AND SCULPTURES

Common themes of Buddhist temple friezes and murals include **Maya's dream**, in which the Buddha's mother saw a white elephant, portending his birth. The **Buddha's birth** is also frequently depicted, as are scenes in which he first sees the cruelties of life outside the privileged world of the royal palace, and leaves the palace for a life of ascetic contemplation, before finally becoming liberated from the cycle of birth and rebirth in the scene called **Mahaparinirvana**.

▼ *Below: The massive sea-facing ramparts of Galle failed to protect the Dutch garrison from English conquest.*

Among the delights of Sri Lankan cooking for the tourist are many kinds of fish and other seafood, from tasty, firm-fleshed deep-sea fish like tuna to lobster, prawn and crab found in abundance in the lagoons and coastal shallows. Smaller fish are often preserved by drying, and Sri Lanka imports tons of dried fish from the tiny Indian Ocean islands of the Maldives archipelago, several hundred miles to the northwest. Strong tasting and strong smelling, these are a local delicacy, but are very much an acquired taste. Squid, cuttlefish and octopus all also make an appearance on the menu, grilled or served in curry.

shape of a dome, the dagoba, usually painted white, often enshrines a relic of the Buddha, such as a hair or a tooth, and is usually massively constructed of brick covered with a coat of plaster.

The pantiled roofs and verandahs which grace many older buildings are the legacy of the Portuguese and Dutch. Galle has many fine old Dutch buildings, while in Kandy and Nuwara Eliya there are many surviving buildings from the British colonial era which would not look out of place in an English country town.

Statues of the Buddha are features of ancient temple sites, where they are often carved from the living rock of basalt crags and cliffs. The Buddha may be represented standing, reclining or sitting in meditation. Carved friezes often show elephants, which symbolize power and wealth, while frescoes like those at Sigiriya may display beautiful women, temple dancers or deities.

FOOD AND DRINK

Sri Lanka is blessed with fertile soil, rich seas and a tropical climate in which delicious fruit, fresh vegetables and flavour-

some spices grow abundantly. That abundance is reflected in the country's cooking, which also shows the influences of the many races who have settled the island of Sri Lanka in past centuries.

Rice and Curry

No traditional meal in Sri Lanka is complete without rice, usually served plainly boiled or steamed and accompanied by any one of dozens of different curry dishes. Usually, a main meal comprises one central curry dish – chicken, lamb, beef, fish or prawn – with a selection of vegetable and *dhal* (lentil) dishes.

Along with these are side dishes of chutney and pickle. Some of these are cooling (such as mango chutney), while others are fiery. Among the spiciest of all Sri Lankan side dishes is *pol sambol*, a potent paste blended from onion, coconut, chilli, lime juice and dried fish and served with rice. Coconut milk is a major ingredient in all Sri Lankan curries, which are generally lighter and less rich than the curry dishes of northern India, and have much in common with the cooking of the Indian south.

Many Sri Lankans, both Hindu and Buddhist, follow a vegetarian diet at least part of the time, and Sri Lanka is an excellent destination for vegetarians, with many delicious meat-free dishes to choose from on the menu.

◀ *Opposite: The silvery catch of the famous stilt-fishermen of Sri Lanka's south coast.*

Spices

The spices which first drew Europeans to the island – cloves, cardamom, nutmeg, cinnamon and pepper – still grow in great abundance in Sri Lanka. They lend richness and zest to many dishes, often in proportions that depend on availability and the chef's personal taste rather than on any fixed recipe.

Drink

Fruit juices are widely available but should be treated with caution as they may not have been blended with water that is safe to drink. Tap water may be contaminated, particularly during the monsoon season. You should be able to trust fruit juices in main resort hotels, but those sold in smaller restaurants and roadside stands are best avoided. Bottled water and soft drinks are widely available.

Grapes are among the few fruits that will not grow in Sri Lanka, so all wines are imported and are therefore relatively expensive and often of indifferent quality. Lion lager, the country's main brand of beer, is relatively expensive in Sri Lankan terms, but like almost everything else in Sri Lanka is cheap by international standards. Imported beers, and Guinness stout brewed under licence, are also available in bars and restaurants in the main tourist areas.

FOREIGN FOOD

Colonial dishes which have stood the test of time include *lampries* – curried rice with meatballs, baked in a banana leaf – which was introduced by the Dutch from the East Indies. British-style roast beef still sometimes appears on the menu, but it is the new empire of tourism that is having the most profound effect on Sri Lankan eateries with Italian, French, and German restaurants appearing in Colombo and in the main holiday resorts. Virtually every Sri Lankan budget restaurant also claims to serve 'Chinese' dishes – usually no more than a handful of rice and noodle dishes such as chow mein and chop suey. Many of the top-end international hotels in Colombo have Japanese, Chinese and North Indian restaurants in addition to their Sri Lankan and international eating places.

2
Colombo

Colombo, Sri Lanka's bustling commercial capital, is located on the country's west coast and with a population of between 800,000 and one million (estimates vary) is by far the country's biggest city, as well as its window on the world. Its natural harbour at the mouth of the Kelani River was a magnet for successive traders and conquerors – first Arab merchants, then Portuguese, Dutch and British imperialists.

The city is a sometimes jarring mix of old and new, with a central cluster of high-rise office blocks and hotels overshadowing red-tiled colonial-era buildings and sprawling street markets which overflow with high-piled fruit and vegetables, colourful silks and cottons, and deliciously fragrant spices.

On its crowded streets stand places of worship symbolic of Sri Lanka's multi-ethnic heritage: graceful Buddhist *viharas*, for instance, stand close to gaudy temples encrusted with Hindu statuary, and Muslim mosques with slender minarets.

Colombo's streets, which buzz with life during the day – when its population is swollen by some 400,000 commuting workers – are virtually empty after nightfall, with little nightlife outside a handful of international-standard hotels.

During the day, however, its colourful street markets, colonial-era buildings, museums and galleries, churches, mosques and temples, and the lovely Viharamahadevi Park with it beautiful trees, make it a great place to explore on foot.

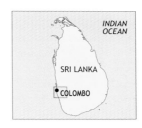

Don't Miss

** **Pettah:** bazaar district packed with shops and stalls.
** **National Museum:** exhibits give insights into life in ancient and modern Sri Lanka.
** **Dutch Period Museum:** glimpse into the vanished era of the Dutch occupation.
* **Viharamahadevi Park:** Colombo's largest and most elegant green space.

◄ *Opposite: The Clock Tower, in Colombo's downtown Fort district.*

COLOMBO

The wettest months in the Colombo region are April, May and June, with rainfall exceeding 350mm (14in) in May; and in October and November when rainfall exceeds 300mm (12in). Maximum temperature is around 30°C (86°F) year-round, with temperatures reaching or exceeding 30°C from January to May and one or two degrees below this level for the rest of the year. **Average temperature** is around **27°C** (81°F).

Originally named **Kolomtota**, Colombo was the main seaport of Kotte, the country's 15th- and 16th-century capital. Known to Arab traders as Kalamba, the city attracted the rapacious Portuguese as early as 1505 and became the bastion of their rule for almost 150 years. Surprisingly little remains to attest to this era, apart from a scattering of Portuguese surnames in the telephone directory and a handful of Roman Catholic churches and seminaries. Nor are there many mementoes of the Dutch who expelled the Portuguese in the mid-17th century. The central area of the city is still known as **Fort**, but the remnants of the colonial battlements have long since been demolished, or incorporated in newer buildings.

There are more mementoes of the British period, including the neoclassical old parliament building, the Victorian-era **President's House** (still often called 'Queen's House'), and the grandly mercantile brick façade of **Cargill's**, a splendid 19th-century department store that has changed little since the 19th-century heyday of Sri Lanka's British tea planters.

FORT

Fort, between Colombo Harbour to the north and the murky urban lagoon of Beira Lake to the south, is the heart of Colombo. The Portuguese built and extended their fortress here during more than a century of conquest and resistance. It was taken over by the Dutch, and finally demolished by the British after they completed their conquest of the country in the mid-19th century. Today, the area is the city's financial and commercial heart and houses Colombo's main international hotels, as well as Sri Lanka's seat of government.

The mid-19th-century **Clock Tower**, at the corner of Janadhipathi Mawatha and Chatham Street, was originally a lighthouse and is now a handy landmark for the city centre area. Other landmarks include the **President's House** and **Presidential Gardens**, a palatial neoclassical building which was originally the home of the British Governors and is now the residence of Sri Lanka's president; it is sadly off limits to visitors.

Between 1995 and the end of the civil war, LTTE bomb attacks in Colombo killed more than 300 people and wounded 2000. At the same time, large numbers of Tamil people from the north moved to Colombo to escape the fighting, and this heightened ethnic rivalries in the capital. Most of the checkpoints built to counter terrorist attacks have been dismantled but you may encounter temporary roadblocks manned by the security forces. While Colombo is now generally peaceful, visitors should be aware that ethnic tensions between Sinhala and Tamil communities in the capital can sometimes be high.

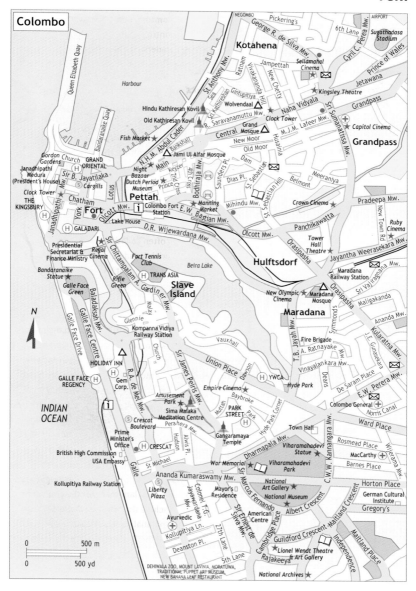

COLOMBO

1. Hindu Kathiresan Kovil
2. Old Kathiresan Kovil
3. Wolvendaal Church
4. Grand Mosque
5. Jami-Ul Alfar Mosque

▶ Right: Wolvendaal Church, built in 1749, is one of the oldest Protestant churches still in use on the island.

Dutch Hospital Shopping Precinct*

This group of 17th century buildings has been transformed into a stylish retail and leisure complex around a courtyard filled with shops, cafes and restaurants.Hospital Lane, Fort; www.uda.lk

PETTAH

Immediately east of Fort (across the narrow canal that separates the outer harbour from the Beira Lake) is Pettah, a maze of streets and alleys piled and crammed with goods of every description, from colourful textiles, gold and silver, and colonial-era antiquities to the necessities of everyday life – spices, fruit and vegetables, reeking heaps of dried fish, paraffin, batteries, electrical goods, clothes and footwear. Whatever you are looking for, you'll find it in Pettah – though shopping here, which can call for determined bargaining, is not for the faint of heart. Among the most interesting streets for both sightseeing and shopping is **Sea Street**, in the north-east corner of Pettah, with its goldsmiths' workshops and the dramatically colourful **Hindu Kathiresan** and **Old Kathiresan** *kovils* (temples). These are the starting point for the Vel festival, celebrating the marriage of the god Murugan (the top Tamil deity) to his queen Deivanai and concubine Vaali Amma, and held each year in August. Not too far from these stand the **Grand Mosque**, the most important mosque for Sri Lanka's Muslim population, on New Moor Street, whose

VEL FESTIVAL

Colombo's main **Hindu festival**, celebrated by the Tamil community, is held during the **August full moon**, when the gorgeously decorated Vel chariot of Skanda, the Hindu god of war, carries his weapons around the Hindu temples of the capital. Skanda, an aspect of Shiva, also has a major temple and pilgrimage site at Kataragama, in southeast Sri Lanka, where pilgrims flock during the July/August Esala pilgrimage season.

very name reflects a long-standing heritage of contact with the Arab world, and the **Jami Ul Alfar Mosque**, at the corner of Bankshall Street and Second Cross Street. Built at the beginning of the 20th century, its decorative brickwork, patterned in red and white, is conspicuous.

Dutch Period Museum **

Built in the 17th century as the residence of Count August van Ranzow, the Dutch East India Company's governor in Colombo, this attractive old building at 95 Prince Street is one of the few surviving remnants of Colombo's Dutch colonial heritage. On the fringes of Pettah, it is surrounded by market stalls and antique shops. Its collection includes coins, weapons, pottery, portraits and furniture from the period of Dutch rule, and also traces the descent of the dwindling 'Burgher' community. Open Saturday–Thursday 09:00–17:00 (www.stichtingnederlandsrilanka.nl).

Wolvendaal Church **

Another relic of the Dutch period is this stone church on Wolvendaal Street, built in 1749. Worth looking at are the **tombstones** set into the floor, which were moved from a church within the Fort in 1813.

The dates on the tombs of several Dutch governors, whose bones were reinterred here, reveal how risky life could be for the Dutch conquerors: even in peacetime, the death toll from disease was high and many died after only a short stay in Colombo. Open during usual church hours (www. wolvendaal.org).

GALLE FACE AREA
Galle Face Green, immediately south of the Fort, is a long, thin park which fills up with food stalls

▼ Below: Shops and stalls in Colombo's crowded Pettah market district overflow with goods of all kinds.

COLOMBO

1. Hindu Kathiresan Kovil
2. Old Kathiresan Kovil
3. Wolvendaal Church
4. Grand Mosque
5. Jami Ul Alfar Mosque

on weekend evenings and is a popular meeting place for local people. A narrow arm of Beira Lake separates this district from **Slave Island**, actually a peninsula where the Dutch imprisoned slaves from their Asian colonies.

Galle Road, Colombo's long seafront boulevard, runs south from Galle Face Green, eventually becoming the main coastal road to Galle and the south. It's always crowded with traffic and short on charm, but as the city's main thoroughfare it also has some of the best shopping and a number of important buildings, including the official residence of Sri Lanka's premier, the US Embassy, the British High Commission and some of the city's top hotels.

Cinnamon Gardens

The Cinnamon Gardens district, approximately a block inland (east) from Galle Road, shows not a trace of the spice plantations from which it gets its name, but is now the city's university and diplomatic quarter and its wealthiest residential area. With its boulevards lined with jacaranda and frangipani trees, it is in sharp contrast to the grime, commerce and visible poverty of the Pettah area to the

CINNAMON

Of all the spices that drew the Dutch to Sri Lanka, cinnamon was the most important. Not content with the piecemeal cultivation traditional to the island, they began systematically setting up plantations, and by the time they were ousted by Britain, in the late 18th century, the island had a monopoly of the world's cinnamon trade. With the British takeover, boom years followed as new markets for the spice opened up, but Britain could not keep a monopoly forever, and by the 1820s other spice-growing countries were in competition and the price of cinnamon plummeted. It is still grown, but is not economically vital.

▶ Right: Colombo's Town Hall, with its colonnades and white dome.

north. The **Town Hall**, the white dome of which is said to have been modelled on that of the Capitol complex of Washington DC, is a major landmark, overlooking the semi-circular expanse of **Viharamahadevi Park**, Colombo's largest and most elegant and attractive green space. The park is at its prettiest from March to May, before the monsoon arrives, when its trees and shrubberies are in brilliant flower. In the centre of the park a statue of **Queen Victoria** commemorates her rule over the island, while on the lawns near the Town Hall a golden image of the **Buddha** represents an even older heritage.

National Museum ★★

At Sir Marcus Fernando Mawatha (also known as Albert Crescent), next to the Viharamahadevi Park, the **National Museum** was Sri Lanka's first and was founded in 1877. Its collection spans several centuries and a range of cultures, from the Sinhala kingdoms through to the British era. Highlights include the royal trappings of the last **Kings of Kandy**. There is also some superb stone sculpture, as well as Hindu bronzes and wooden carvings, Sri Lankan and European furniture and ceramics, and (to Western eyes) a fine array of grotesque masks representing Buddhist demons and deities. The museum's huge **library** of more than 500,000 books is primarily of interest to scholars, but some of its collection of 4000 palm leaf manuscripts – created by etching the lettering into the fibrous surface of the leaf – are on display. A small **gallery** of mid-19th-century paintings and etchings shows Sri Lanka through the eyes of British artists.

The museum's Anuradhapura period, prehistoric, coins

▲ Above: Puppetry plays a significant role in Sri Lanka's culture and history. Puppets like these can be seen at the Traditional Puppet Art Museum.

OLA MANUSCRIPTS

Palm-leaf was used by the Kandyan kings and earlier rulers to record royal decrees, genealogies, histories and religious scriptures. The tough leaves were cut into strips and then inscribed by cutting letters into the green outer layer of the leaf to reveal the tough inner fibre. The dried strips were then stitched together to create a manuscript that looks like a miniature Venetian blind covered with curling characters.

and currency and arms and armaments sections closed for renovation in 2014 and will remain so until further notice. Open Saturday–Thursday, 09:00–17:00 (www.museum.gov.lk).

Natural History Museum *

This old-fashioned collection is a hit and miss affair with stuffed birds and animals displayed in cases showing their natural habitat, and sections dealing with Sri Lanka's geology, climate, and plant life. The most striking display is of an **elephant's skeleton**, and there are also displays which focus on some of the country's ambitious hydro-electric and irrigation engineering schemes. Open 09:00–17:00 daily.

Traditional Puppet Art Museum**

This small, privately run museum aims to keep the art of puppetry and puppet-making alive and has a collection of traditional and contemporary puppets. There are video shows and occasional live performances. 39-40 Anagarika Dharmapala Mawatha, tel: 011 271 44214, www.puppet.lk Open 09:00–17:00 daily.

AROUND COLOMBO

Colombo's vast urban sprawl has pushed the city limits northwards in the direction of Negombo (where the city's Bandaranaike International Airport is located) and southwards towards Mount Lavinia. These residential suburbs and resort areas have the beaches closest to the city centre, and as a result were the first to be developed for **beach tourism**. Both areas, however, have been overtaken by more attractive resorts with better beaches in the southwest. They have also suffered from the slump in tourism caused by the civil war from the late 1980s onwards, and many of the big **resort hotels** built here in anticipation of an ongoing tourism boom are as a result somewhat under-used and very affordable.

DEHIWALA ZOO

The big deal at the Dehiwala Zoo at Allen Avenue, in the suburb of Dehiwala, 10km (6 miles) south of the city centre, is the daily **elephant show**, with a troop of trained elephants being put through their paces. Whether you enjoy this will depend on how you feel about performing animals. Open daily 08:00–18:00, elephant show 17:00 daily.

Negombo ★★

For a shorter beach holiday, or as a stopover on your first or last night in Sri Lanka, Negombo, 37km (23 miles) north of Colombo city centre, has the virtue of being the closest beach resort to Bandaranaike International Airport. For that reason, it also appears in a number of tour operator brochures. Nicknamed 'Little Rome' because of its numerous Catholic churches – a survival from the period of Portuguese rule – Negombo surrounds a **lagoon** which is rich in fish and until the advent of tourism provided most of the villagers with a living. Today, tourism provides a ready market for the lagoon's prawns and lobsters, and for deepwater fish like tuna, shark and amber-jack, but the picturesque twin-hulled sailing canoes are slowly being ousted by modern wooden or plastic-hulled, motor-driven boats. Nevertheless, the narrow streets and colourful stucco churches of the old part of town make Negombo acceptably picturesque for a short stay, and there are more than a dozen luxury resort hotels to choose from.

Negombo's **beach** is less than brilliant by Sri Lankan standards – there are other, far better beaches elsewhere – and the sea is often murky as a result of silt carried into it from the 12km (7.5-mile) lagoon, but it suffered relatively little tsunami damage.

COLOMBO WETLANDS

Only 7km (4 miles) from the airport, just off the main Colombo–Negombo road, the **Muthurajawela Marshes** are Sri Lanka's first wetlands reserve, with **boat rides** from the visitor centre through a wide expanse of marshland which connects with the Negombo Lagoon. Birds to be seen include purple herons, egrets, four kingfisher species, grebes, moorhens, lesser whistling ducks, and painted storks, while toque monkeys may also be seen from the boat. The marshlands also shelter 15 amphibian species, 37 reptile species and 34 mammal species.

▼ *Below: Fishing boats like this outrigger vessel on the lagoon at Negombo, north of Colombo, have changed little over centuries.*

COLOMBO

Dutch Fort *

Commanding the entrance to the lagoon, the ruined Dutch Fort dates from 1678, according to the date inscribed above its stone gateway. It was built some 34 years after the Dutch wrested Sri Lanka from Portugal, and defended the natural harbour from which the Dutch East India Company exported cinnamon and other spices, which were the island's most valuable exports. Next to the walls is a Dutch cemetery. Open during daylight hours.

St Mary's Church **

This is the most picturesque of the town's many Catholic churches and chapels, and is a testimony to the enthusiasm with which the local Karava people adopted Catholicism under Portuguese tutelage. The **painted ceiling** is well worth a look. It is open during the usual church hours.

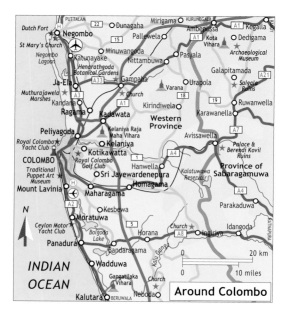

Around Colombo

Mount Lavinia *

Situated approximately 11km (6 miles) south of Colombo city centre, Mount Lavinia has a beach with a potentially dangerous undertow and occasionally polluted waters which diminish the appeal of its golden sands and swaying palms. Much of its reputation rests on the charm of the **Mount Lavinia Hotel**.

In around 1805–6 the then British Governor, **Sir Thomas Maitland**, built an official residence here, naming it after his mistress. It was rebuilt between 1823 and 1827 by one of his successors, Edward Barnes; it became a government rest house in 1877 and was converted into a hotel in 1895.

Modern additions have obliterated much of its old-world charm, despite several attempts to maintain some continuity with its past. A **superb swimming pool** with great sea views makes up for the deficiencies of the beach.

Kalutara *

This bustling village at the mouth of the Kalu Ganga, about 45km (27 miles) south of Colombo, was, like Negombo, a very important entrepôt for the cinnamon and nutmeg trades but is now better known for its **coconut palm gardens** and for coconut-fibre mats, rope and baskets. Kalutara also claims to produce the tastiest **mangosteens** in Sri Lanka.

The town is recovering well after the waves, with flooding rather than destruction being the main problem, and much of the tourism infrastructure is now operational.

Basket Centre *

The Basket Centre is located in the middle of the village. You can see baskets and other wares being woven from coconut fibre, with the opportunity to buy. The tough, well-made baskets come in handy if you haven't enough space in your luggage for all your other souvenir purchases, and they are wonderful gifts as well. Open 08:00–17:00 daily.

Gangatilaka Vihara *

On the banks of the Kalu Ganga, next to the road bridge, stands the Gangatilaka Vihara, a large dagoba (Buddhist shrine) beside which stands a sacred bo-tree. The hollow dagoba has an unusual **painted interior**, and windows affording beautiful views of the river. It is open during daylight hours. If you intend to go inside, a small cash offering, to be placed in the box fixed to the sacred tree, will be appreciated.

Durutu Perahera

Peraheras, or Buddhist religious processions, are held at important temples all over Sri Lanka. The *Durutu Perahera*, held during the month of January, with the day determined by the full moon of that month, takes place at the **Kelaniya Temple**, 12km (8 miles) east of Colombo city centre near the suburb of Kotte, with torch bearers, drummers and brightly caparisoned Asian elephants.

COLOMBO AT A GLANCE

BEST TIMES TO VISIT

Colombo is most pleasant from Sept to late Apr. From May to Sept, the **southwest monsoon** deposits heavy rain on the west coast and heavy seas make swimming dangerous at Negombo and Mount Lavinia.

GETTING THERE

By air: International scheduled flights by national carrier SriLankan Airlines and other European carriers from Amsterdam, London, Frankfurt and other European cities, mostly via Dubai. Direct connections to Delhi, Mumbai, Singapore and other Asian capitals. SriLankan Airlines also flies to the Maldives. International flight information, tel: 011 225 2861, www.airport.lk Cinnamon Air, (tel: 011 247 5475, www.cinnamonair.com) operates floatplane flights between Colombo and Bentota, Kandy, Dickwella, Kogalla, Trincomalee and Sigiriya.

By rail: Sri Lanka Railways (www.railways.gov.lk) runs trains from Fort Railway Station, tel: 011 243 2908, in central Colombo to points including Kandy, Trincomalee, Anuradhapura, Galle and Matara. Rail service between Colombo and Jaffna resumed in 2014 after a 24-year hiatus.

By road: Coach services operate from Colombo to points throughout Sri Lanka, with some air-conditioned express services. Central Bus Stand, Olcott Mawatha, Colombo 11, information, tel: 011 232 9604.

GETTING AROUND

Car hire: Self-drive cars are available through **Avis**, tel: 011 438 5405, www.avis.com but a car with driver is preferable. These are also available through Avis and tour agencies.

Trains: Local trains run from Colombo Fort Station to the southern suburbs, including Dehiwala and Mount Lavinia, and to the airport. Railway information, tel: 011 243 2908.

Buses: Buses are cheap and frequent, but can be crowded and uncomfortable, especially in early morning and evening rush hour. Services to all suburban points leave from stops near the Fort Railway Station. Central Bus Stand information, tel: 011 232 9604—6.

Taxis: Taxis are a bargain and by far the best way of getting around unless you are on a really tight budget. Air-conditioned, metered cabs are available from GNTC, tel: 011 268 8688, and Kangaroo Cabs, tel: 011 258 8588.

Three-wheelers: A hybrid of motor scooter and rickshaw, these mini taxis go everywhere but are unmetered and charge tourists double the local fare. They are cheap if you agree on a price before you get in.

WHERE TO STAY

There are many comfortably bland international chain hotels in central Colombo, complemented by a growing portfolio of charming small boutique hotels.

Central Colombo
Luxury

Galadari Hotel, 64 Lotus Road, Echelon Square, tel: 011 254 4544, fax: 011 244 9875, www.galadarihotel.lk The best value five-star in town, with nightclub and large-screen TV.

The Kingsbury, 48 Janadhipathi Mawatha, Colombo 1, tel: 011 242 1221, www.thekingsbury.lk Comfortable hotel with large pool and fine sea views.

Galle Face Hotel & Galle Face Regency, 2 Galle Road, Colombo, tel: 011 254 1010, www.gallefacehotel.com The grand old lady of Colombo hotels, built at the height of the colonial era. Its south wing was refurbished in 2005 as a separate, luxury boutique hotel.

Park Street Hotel, 20 Park Street, Colombo 2, tel: 011 576 9500, www.parkstreethotel-colombo.com Elegant, new boutique hotel; 12 designer rooms in a lovely old mansion; with pool and other luxuries.

Casa Colombo, 231 Galle Rd, tel: 011 452 0130, www.casacolombo.com Very chic boutique address, one of the most stylish new places to stay in the capital, with 12 suites in a 200-year-old 'Moorish' house.

Mid-range
Havelock Place Bungalow, 6—8 Havelock Place, Colombo 5, tel: 011 258 5191, www.havelockbungalow.com Lovely, nostalgic rooms and suites (seven in all) in two

vintage bungalows, furnished with antiques, set in lush gardens, and embellished facilities such as pool and Jacuzzi.

Negombo
Mid-range
Paradise Beach Hotel,
tel: 011 587 3305, www.
paradisebeachsrilanka.com
Mid-sized holiday hotel on the beach, 15 minutes from the airport, with pool, restaurant, bar and other modern facilities.

WHERE TO EAT
Colombo offers a tremendous and ever-expanding choice of places to eat, from affordable family restaurants in the city and along Marine Drive and Galle Face to fine-dining establishments within posh hotels. For reviews, see the *Daily Mirror* newspaper or its online edition (www.daily mirror.lk), or visit www.lanka restaurants.com which lists and reviews restaurants all over Sri Lanka.

Luxury
Sea Spray Restaurant, Galle Face Hotel, tel: 011 254 1010. Upscale seafood restaurant. Immaculate service.

Mid-range
Ministry of Crab, Old Dutch Hospital Shopping Precinct, tel: 011 234 2722, www.ministryofcrab.com It's all about the crabs and other seafood at this trendy eating place in Colombo's newest dining hotspot.

Budget
New Banana Leaf Restaurant, 720 Galle Road, tel: 011 731 6666. Reincarnation of much loved eatery, still serving Sri Lankan food the traditional way. Locals rave about the chicken biryani.
MB Yaal, 56 Vaverset Place, Marine Drive, tel: 011 754 8888. This family-run restaurant serves signature food from Jaffna, including dishes such as odiyal cool, fish perratal, thirrukal pittu and kanawa kottu.

SHOPPING
Laksala (the Sri Lanka Handicrafts Board) has its flagship store, the **Laksala Emporium**, at 60 York Street in Colombo's Fort district, open 09:30–17:00 weekdays and 09:00–16:00 Saturdays. Good buys include silverware, brasswork, rattan, lacquer, carved woodwork, demon masks and more, all made by artisans trained at Laksala's network of craft schools which aim to provide employment and keep traditional skills alive. The organization also has more than 20 outlets nationwide, in Galle, Kandy and other popular tourist spots; *see* laksala.gov.lk for locations. Sri Lanka is famed for its gems, including blue and

star sapphires, rubies, and numerous semiprecious stones such as topaz and amethyst. Crooked vendors try to pass off flawed stones or fakes; genuine stones are sold at the official **Sri Lanka Gem and Jewellery Exchange**, 310 Galle Road, Colombo 3, tel: 011 257 6144, which also offers a valuation and authentication service for stones from other dealers. A list of other officially approved gem dealers is also available from the National Gem and Jewellery Authority (25 Galle Face Terrace, Colombo 3).

TOURS AND EXCURSIONS
Colombo City Tour, tel: 011 281 4700, www.colombo citytours.com Open-topped double-decker bus tours by day and night.
Colombo City Walks, tel: 011 779 9778, www.trekurious. com Guided walks through the historic Fort area.

USEFUL CONTACTS
Sri Lanka Tourism, Colombo Travel Information Centre, 80 Galle Road, Colombo 3, tel: 011 243 7759, www.srilanka.travel
International Airport Travel Information Centre, Colombo, tel: 011 225 2411.

COLOMBO	J	F	M	A	M	J	J	A	S	O	N	D
AVERAGE TEMP. ºC	26	27	27	28	29	27	27	27	27	27	26	26
AVERAGE TEMP. ºF	79	81	81	82	83	81	81	81	81	81	79	79
RAINFALL in	3.5	2.7	5.8	9.1	14.6	8.8	5.3	4.3	6.3	13.7	12.4	5.8
RAINFALL mm	89	69	147	231	371	224	135	109	160	348	315	147
DAYS OF RAINFALL	7	6	8	14	19	18	12	11	13	19	16	10

3
Kandy and the Hill Country

For many, the ancient highland capital of Kandy is still the true heart of Sri Lanka, where the last **Sri Lankan kings** held out against the European powers, protected by the natural defences of their steep hills and dense tropical forests. Portuguese expeditions reached Kandy in the late 16th century, only to be trapped and put to the sword. The more pragmatic Dutch reduced the Kandyan kingdom by blockading its supply routes, but Kandy was finally ceded and its last king captured by the British in 1815.

The journey of 115km (73 miles) inland from Colombo takes up to three hours by rail or road, and as your vehicle crosses deep river valleys, negotiates numerous hairpin bends and winds upward through increasingly steep **hill country** – where cinnamon and nutmeg plantations scent the breeze, tame elephants trudge by under heavy burdens, and flying foxes like ragged umbrellas hang from high branches – it is easy to see how Kandy maintained its independence for so long. In fact, its kings banned the build-ing of roads to the coast, to hinder would-be European conquerors still further. 'The ways are many but very narrow, so that but one can go abreast,' wrote **Robert Knox**, the Scots venturer who was held captive in Kandy for 20 years in the late 17th century.

Surrounded by cool, lush mountain scenery, Kandy is the gateway to a very different aspect of Sri Lanka, one which those visitors who restrict their stay to the country's coastal resorts never see.

INDIAN OCEAN

SRI LANKA

Matale
• Kandy
Nuwara Eliya •   • Badulla
•
Ratnapura

Don't Miss

*** Temple of the Tooth (Dalada Maligawa): this major pilgrimage site guards the sacred tooth relic of the Buddha.
*** Royal Botanical Gardens: beautiful gardens laid out for kings.
*** Pinnawala Elephant Orphanage: herd of rescued elephants meets the public.
*** Horton Plains National Park: high plains landscapes and unique flora and fauna.

◄ *Opposite: The Peradeniya Botanical Gardens, founded by a Kandyan king.*

KANDY AND THE HILL COUNTRY

KANDY PERAHERA

The magnificent *perahera* (procession) – when a replica of the casket that contains the Buddha's tooth is paraded through the streets of Kandy by whirling, colourfully dressed dancers, musicians, acrobats and drummers and a troop of up to 100 elephants caparisoned in silver and crimson – dates back to 1775. Held annually, usually in August, *poya* (worship) lasts for ten days and nights, with the procession going through more streets each night.

South of Kandy, the country rises still further, to the cool green slopes of Sri Lanka's tea country around **Nuwara Eliya**, beneath the country's highest peak, **Pidurutalagala**. Here, the hills rise to an average height of more than 900m (2952ft), with several summits which rise to more than 2000m (6562ft). With its waterfalls, caves and lush woodland sheltering unique animal, bird and butterfly species, this region is a delight for walkers and explorers with an interest in Sri Lanka's natural wonders as well as its ancient cultural heritage.

KANDY

At 500m (1640ft) above sea level, Sri Lanka's second city has a climate that comes as a pleasantly cool contrast to hot and humid Colombo. Amid lush green fields and plantations – evidence of the region's well-watered fertility – the city stands within a loop of the **Mahaweli Ganga**, one of Sri

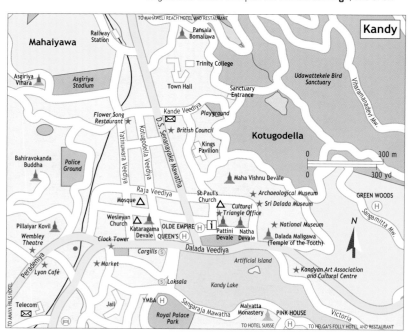

Lanka's more substantial rivers, on the north shore of Kandy Lake, an artificial reservoir completed in 1807, during the reign of the last king of Kandy, Sri Wickrama Rajasinha. He kept his concubines on the artificial island in the centre of the lake, and had a number of his enemies drowned slowly, tied to stakes and gasping for air as the waters of the lake rose.

Temple of the Tooth (Dalada Maligawa) ★★★

Overlooking the north shore of **Kandy Lake**, in the centre of town, the Temple of the Tooth is a place of pilgrimage for millions of devout Buddhists from all over Sri Lanka, and is regarded by Buddhist Sri Lankans as the treasury of their entire culture. Sri Lanka's premiers and presidents traditionally deliver their first post-election speeches from its balcony, and lesser politicians too make thanksgiving visits to the temple on election.

The **Tooth Relic** itself is claimed to have come to Sri Lanka some 1600 years ago, when a certain princess from southern India brought it to Anuradhapura, which was then the most powerful kingdom in Sri Lanka. As kings and kingdoms rose and fell, it finally ended up in Kandy around AD1100. Over centuries, as the Sinhalese came under increasing pressure from invasion, it became more and more symbolic of Sri Lankan freedom and independence.

The existing temple was begun in 1687 and added to by a succession of Kandyan kings over the next 95 years. Painted pale rose, surrounded by walls adorned with elephant carvings and a moat, and roofed with terracotta tiles, the temple receives a steady flow of pilgrims and tourists (www.sridaladamaligawa.lk).

▲ *Above: Temple of the Tooth has a wonderful location overlooking Kandy Lake.*

CLIMATE

The rainiest months in the highlands are June to December, when rainfall at Nuwara Eliya reaches or exceeds 200mm (8in), reaching a high of 300mm (12in) in July. Maximum temperature hovers around 22°C (72°F) year-round, reaching or exceeding 30°C from January to May and one or two degrees below this level for the rest of the year. **Average temperature** is noticeably cooler than on the coast, at only 16°C (61°F) in Kandy and as low as 10°C (50°F) in Nuwara Eliya, thanks to cool night-time temperatures.

▲ *Above: The Temple of the Tooth at Kandy shelters one of the holiest relics of the Buddha in the entire world, and attracts pilgrims from all over the world.*

Dress modestly (no shorts or singlets) and leave your shoes at the entrance before joining the long line that shuffles through the decorated halls and into the darkened, gilt-roofed relic chamber which is the temple's holy of holies. Within, two monks stand sentinel before a gold reliquary, all that you will be allowed to see of the holy molar. Don't, however, miss the **library** of *ola* (palm-leaf) manuscripts in the pagoda-like **moat tower**. The temple is open daily 24 hours; the library is open 09:00–17:00 daily.

Sri Dalada Museum ★★★

Located in the Aluth Maligawa wing of the temple complex, this museum houses documents, royal garments, and artifacts used in the daily Tooth Relic ceremonies, caskets, Buddha images, gem-studded gold and silver bracelets and necklaces, ancient flags, carved ivory tusks, and other royal and sacred relics. Open daily 09:00–17:00. To avoid long queues, buy your admission tickets online.

Kandy National Museum ★★

Next to the Temple, this museum contains royal thrones, sceptres and swords, dating from 17th and 18th centuries. A former palace for the royal concubines, it was here that the Kandyan chiefs surrendered to the British in 1815. Open 09:00–17:00 Sun–Thur (www.museum.gov.lk).

TEMPLE TUSKERS

Sri Lanka's most famous elephant stands in his own museum within the grounds of the Tooth Temple, next to the National Museum. Raja, who died in 1988, carried the temple's sacred relic casket on annual Perahera processions for some 50 years. On his death, he was preserved by the taxidermist's art. Tuskers such as Raja are venerated in Sri Lanka, and those kept at the Tooth Temple are a major attraction for throngs of local people and international visitors. Organisations such as the Born Free foundation have expressed concern for the welfare of these and other captive elephants in Sri Lanka.

Trinity College Chapel *

Trinity College, standing in manicured grounds off D S Senanayake Mawatha, was founded in 1872 to provide education on English lines for the children of British planters and administrators and for Sri Lankan converts to the Anglican church. It is still one of the country's foremost Christian educational establishments. The chapel, with its granite columns carved with traditional Sinhalese patterns as well as the crests of Oxford and Cambridge colleges, is a remarkable blend of western and Sinhalese architectural influences, with wooden doorways and roof beams carved by local craftsmen, a pantiled roof, and overhanging eaves that echo the design of the Tooth Temple. The work of the college's vice principal, it was begun in 1922 to mark the 50th anniversary of the foundation of Trinity College. The huge murals within, depicting stories from the Bible, are the work of the aptly named **David Paynter**, one of Sri Lanka's most famous artists. (www.trinitycollege.lk)

ROBERT KNOX

The son of a Scottish merchant adventurer, the master of the frigate *Anne*, Robert Knox was taken prisoner with his father when their ship landed for repairs at Trincomalee, and was held captive by the King of Kandy, Rajasinha II, from 1660–80. His account of that time, *An Historical Relation of Ceylon*, was published in 1681 and is still one of the authoritative sources on the kingdom of Kandy before its conquest by Britain.

▼ *Below: A sign of commitment at the Udawattekele Bird Sanctuary.*

Udawattekele Bird Sanctuary **

About 1km (0.6 miles) east of Trinity College, off Wewelpitiya Road, this is one of Sri Lanka's more accessible bird sanctuaries. It is a stretch of wilderness only a stone's throw from the city centre with towering forest giants and creepers giving shelter to bird species including Layard's parakeet, Sri Lanka hanging parrot, yellow-fronted barbet, black-capped bulbul, emerald dove, three species of kingfisher, chestnut-headed bee eater and Tickells's blue flycatcher. It is also the home of macaque monkeys, and vividly painted butterflies float across the paths. Open daily 08:00–17:30.

KANDY AND THE HILL COUNTRY

Royal Botanical Gardens ★★★

About 6km (4 miles) southwest of the town centre at Peradeniya on the Colombo highway, close to the banks of the Mahaweli Ganga, these gorgeous gardens were first planted and laid out for King Kirthi Sri Rajasingha (1747–80) and cover some 60ha (150 acres) of trees, lawns and flowering shrubs, including a 20ha (50-acre) **arboretum** of more than 10,000 trees. Under British rule, the royal park became a botanical garden in 1821 and is the largest of Sri Lanka's three main botanical gardens. Here, exotic crops such as coffee, tea, nutmeg, rubber and cinchona (quinine) – all of which later became important to Sri Lanka's economy – were tested. Sights include a **palm avenue** planted by the British in 1905. Another British import was the enormous spreading **Java fig** which sprawls across the lawn, grown from a sapling brought from the East Indies.

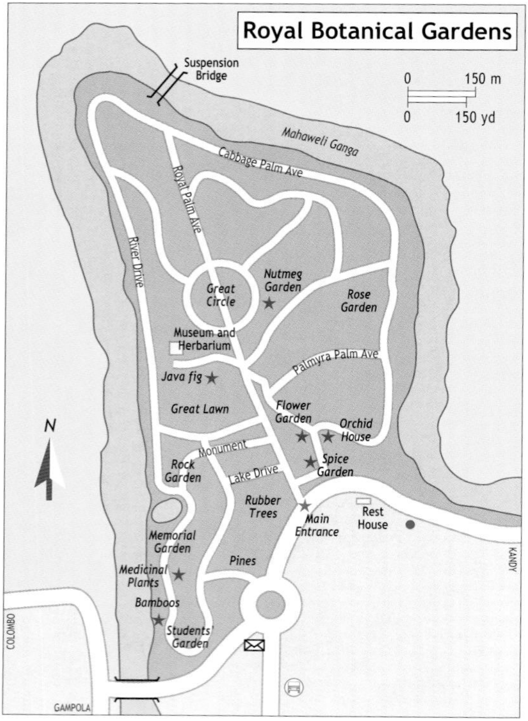

The gardens also have stands of towering **bamboos** from Burma, Japan, China and the East Indies, and a fine collection of **orchids** from Sri Lanka and further afield.

In the centre of the gardens is an **artificial lake** in the shape of the island of Sri Lanka, beside which a white-domed rotunda commemorates George Gardner, superintendent of the gardens in the mid-19th century. Open daily from 07:30 until 17:00, www.botanicgardens.gov.lk

Royal Botanical Gardens

Suspension Bridge

0   150 m
0   150 yd

Mahaweli Ganga

Cabbage Palm Ave

Royal Palm Ave

River Drive

Great Circle

Nutmeg Garden

Rose Garden

Museum and Herbarium

Palmyra Palm Ave

Java fig ★

Great Lawn

Flower Garden

Orchid House

Spice Garden

Monument

Rock Garden

Lake Drive

Rubber Trees

Main Entrance

Rest House

Memorial Garden

Medicinal Plants

Pines

Bamboos

Students' Garden

N

COLOMBO

GAMPOLA

KANDY

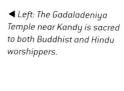

◄ Left: The Gadaladeniya Temple near Kandy is sacred to both Buddhist and Hindu worshippers.

AROUND KANDY

The lush countryside around Kandy is dotted with small Buddhist and Hindu shrines and temples, while just off the Colombo highway, the Pinnewala Elephant Orphanage is well worth stopping at on the way to or from Kandy. A small donation (usually anything from 20 to 100 rupees) is required to visit the temples.

Embekke Devale ★

About 6km (4 miles) southwest of Peradeniya and 3km (2 miles) east of the main road to Nuwara Eliya, around 13km (8 miles) from the centre of Kandy, this small Buddhist temple dates from the 14th century and is graced by **wooden columns** elaborately sculpted with birds, dancers, acrobats and wrestlers. It is open during daylight hours.

Lankatilake Temple ★

Just under 2km (1.5 miles) north of the Embekke Temple, the Lankatilake Temple is predominantly a Hindu place of worship but also has Buddhist **frescoes**, a **Buddha** image,

ESALA FESTIVAL

The **full moon day** of Esala (July/August) is the high point of ten nights of drumming, dancing and processions, with Kandyan dancers and drummers in traditional costume, chiefs in medieval court dress, and more than a hundred elephants in colourful trappings parading through the streets of Kandy, Sri Lanka's hill capital, in a vivid re-enactment of life in the central highlands before the British conquest.

KANDY AND THE HILL COUNTRY

and stone **elephant** carvings. It is open during daylight hours only.

Gadaladeniya Temple ★
Approximately 3km (2 miles) on foot or by bus north of Lankatilake, and 1km (0.6 miles) south of the main Colombo road, this is a mainly Buddhist temple with a Hindu shrine attached. It contains some interesting **Buddha images** and **frescoes** from the 14th century. Open during daylight hours.

Pinnawala Elephant Orphanage ★★★
A visit to the elephant orphanage near Kegalla, 20km (12 miles) west of Kandy on the Colombo highway, where young **orphaned** or **abandoned elephants** are cared for, is a must. The herd usually numbers about 50, from tiny infants (tiny in elephant terms, that is) to hefty adolescents and young adults. Most have lost their parents either to poachers or road accidents, but some have simply become separated from their parental herd. Habituated to humans and domestic elephants, most of the orphans remain in captivity when they reach maturity as they cannot easily be returned to the wild.

The elephant orphanage is open daily, from dawn to dusk. Elephant bathing times are 10:00 and 14:00 daily, and feeding times are 09:00 and 13:00.

On the road from the highway to the orphanage, look out for the scores of **flying foxes** (fruit bats) hanging high in the treetops beside the river or, at sunset, spreading their wings.

NUWARA ELIYA

Nuwara Eliya, situated approximately 100km (62 miles) south of Kandy and among some of Sri Lanka's most verdant hillsides at 1800m (5906ft) above sea level, is more reminiscent of the days of the **English tea planters** than any other place in Sri Lanka.

With mountain forests, wilderness areas and national parks in easy reach – starting only 8km (5 miles) from the centre – Nuwara Eliya is a very popular base for bird-watchers and ecotourists. It also has an adequate 18-hole golf course.

CEYLON TEA

Sri Lankan tea – still exported as 'Ceylon' tea despite the country's change of name in 1972 – is one of Sri Lanka's **main exports** and is available everywhere. Teas grown in the highest plantations, at up to 2000m (6562ft) above sea level, have the highest reputation. Tea may be served black, with lemon, or with boiled milk, while in budget eating places 'milk tea' – a sticky sweet concoction of sugar, tea and condensed milk – is the favourite version.

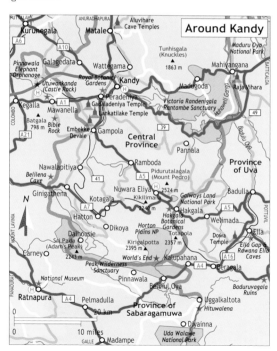

◄ *Opposite: Elephants at the Pinnawala Elephant Orphanage enjoy a daily bath with their trainers in the muddy waters of the nearby river.*

KANDY AND THE HILL COUNTRY

► Right: Bear monkeys are among three monkey species found in Sri Lanka's forests.

Victoria Park ★

This ornamental park located in the centre of town is a pleasant place for a walk. It ia also popular with birders in search of Himalayan migrants such as pied thursh, Kashmir flycatcher, Indian blue robin and Indian pitta, as well as highland endemics such as yellow-eared bulbul. Open daily.

Galways Land National Park

A few kilometres from the town centre, it provides access to visitors who would like to experience a highland forest, though it's nearly 2km (1.2 miles) of footpath. Open daily.

Pidurutalagala ★

Sri Lanka's highest peak, also known as Mount Pedro, rises 2524m (8281ft) above sea level, immediately behind the town. Unfortunately, the path to the summit, which is the site of Sri Lanka's main television transmitter, is closed to visitors for security reasons. For a view of the summit, and a superb panorama of the surrounding hills and plantations, you can walk to the top of the picturesquely named **Single Tree Mountain**, south of the town off the Badulla road, in about 90 minutes.

Hakgala Botanical Gardens ★★

After the Royal Botanical Gardens at Peradeniya, Hakgala, 10km (6 miles) south of Nuwara Eliya, is the second most important garden in Sri Lanka. Though on a smaller scale than those at Peradeniya, Hakgala's plantations of roses, shrubs, ferns and montane woodland are delightfully located, with scenic views. Open daily from 07:30 to 17:00 (www.botanicgardens.gov.lk).

Above the gardens, a forest trail leads into **virgin woodland** – the home of a troop of purple-faced leaf monkeys, a species endemic to Sri Lanka, and to endemic bird species including the Sri Lanka white-eye, Sri Lanka wood pigeon, and Sri Lanka whistling thrush.

Horton Plains National Park ★★★

Declared a UNESCO World Heritage Site in 2010, the land-scapes of this high, misty plateau, some 20km (12 miles) south of Nuwara Eliya and up to 2400m (7874ft) above sea level, are unique in Sri Lanka, combining mountain grassland with areas of miniature 'elfin' forest – dwarf forms of trees and shrubs adapted to the cool climate and skimpy soil of the plains. Above the plateau rise the summits of **Kirigalpotta** and **Totapola**, at 2395m (7858ft) and 2357m (7733ft) respectively, they are Sri Lanka's second- and third-highest peaks.

Wildlife includes sambar, which keep to the edge of wooded areas, bear monkey, often seen and heard in forested areas, and giant squirrel and leopard, which are shy and very rarely seen. Many visitors make a beeline for **World's End**, the 900m (2953ft) drop-off that forms an abrupt southern boundary to the plains. For the best views, arrive at sunrise, before the mist that often shrouds the slopes below has had time to form.

RUBBER

Rubber, still an important crop which accounts for **3 per cent of Sri Lanka's exports**, came to the island from its native South America by way of Kew Gardens near London, where British botanists raised thousands of seedlings from seeds smuggled out of Brazil to break the Brazilian monopoly on rubber. The first rubber trees were planted in the 1890s and by 1901 some 1012ha (2500 acres) of land in the foothills of the central highlands were planted in rubber. Today, more than 242,816ha (600,000 acres) is devoted to growing rubber.

KANDY AND THE HILL COUNTRY

SRI PADA

Thousands of devout believers – mainly Buddhists, but also Hindus, Muslims and Christians – climb Sri Pada (**Adam's Peak**) during the pilgrimage season each year. Observances start on the full moon day of December and continue until the full moon day of April the following year. **Sunrise**, seen from the peak, is one of the great sights of Sri Lanka, but making the climb during pilgrimage season takes many hours longer than doing it in other months.

Knuckles Conservation Forest ★★★

The Knuckles Range, with more than 30 peaks over 900m (3000ft) in height (the highest, Gombariya, rises to 1906m/6248ft), is a unique ecosystem bounded in the east by the Mahaveli River system and to the west by the Matale plains. The area has been designated as part of the Central Highlands of Sri Lanka World Heritage Property (www.forestdept.gov.lk). The Knuckles Range Nature Centre at Pitawala, near Ilukkumbura, offers a overview of the region, its wildlife, and the way of life of the people who live in its mountain villages.

Adam's Peak (Sri Pada) & Peak Wilderness Sanctuary ★★★

Horton Plains National Park borders the Peak Wilderness Sanctuary, a crescent, 40km (25-mile) swathe of montane forest that can be approached from Dalhousie, 25km (15 miles) west of Nuwara Eliya, off the main Nuwara Eliya–Colombo road, or from Carney, 8km (5 miles) north of Ratnapura.

Adam's Peak, in the centre of the sanctuary, is recog-

▶ Right: The red-wattled lapwing, one of the many rare and endemic bird species found in Sri Lanka's wetlands and fields.

nized as a sacred place by all Sri Lanka's religions. Muslims and some Christians say the 'footprint' in the rock atop the rust-red, 2243m (7359ft) peak is where Adam first set foot on earth after being exiled from Eden. Other Christians say it is the footprint of St Thomas, who brought Christianity to southern India in the 1st century AD, while to Hindus it is the mark of Lord Shiva. Buddhists, however, who have covered the original 'print' with a larger than life concrete copy, say it was made by the Buddha on his third visit to Sri Lanka. In the pilgrimage season, from December until April, thousands trek to the top each day, taking all day to complete the 8km (5-mile) ascent from Dalhousie village. At other times, the ascent will take you around four hours.

RATNAPURA

Roughly 100km (64 miles) southeast of Colombo, Ratnapura is known as Sri Lanka's gemstone capital. The town has fine views of Adam's Peak. Precious stones are dug by hand from small pockets of gem-bearing gravel in the hills and fields around Ratnapura, and include sapphires, rubies, moonstones, and semiprecious stones such as zircon, garnet and quartz, all of which you will be offered on the street by shady looking characters offering a 'special price'. As many naive buyers have found, there are no bargains and many ripoffs. Even in legitimate gem vendors' stores, prices are not necessarily lower than in your home country (and you will have to pay import tax on your return home). Precious and semi-precious stones are also sold loose by more reputable stores; to get the best price, don't buy from the first shop you see — look around first.

Ratnapura National Museum ★

Housed in Ehelapola Walauwa mansion, the Ratnapura National Museum explores the morphology of gem landscapes and also displays ancient animal skeletons found during mining operations. The museum is open 09:00–17:00 Sat–Wed (www.museum.gov.lk).

Buying Gems

The best and safest way to buy Sri Lankan gemstones is at the government-run Gem and Jewellery Exchange in Colombo, which is operated by the National Gem and Jewellery Authority to assist the export of precious stones. The Exchange also has a gem-testing laboratory and assay centre, so you can find out if any stones you have bought are the real thing. *See* Colombo At a Glance, Shopping, p. 45.

Best Times to Visit

The hill country is most pleasant from Sept to late Apr. From May to Sept, heavy rains make travel slower and less easy and visiting the mainly open-air attractions of the region less appealing.

Getting There

By rail: Trains run between Colombo Fort Railway Station and Kandy up to nine times daily. Trains also connect Kandy with Nanu Oya (for Nuwara Eliya) and Ohiya (for Horton Plains), on a loop that ends at Badulla, on the eastern fringe of the hill country. Train information and reservations: Fort Railway Station, tel: 011 243 2908; Kandy Railway Station, tel: 081 222 2271; www.railway.gov.lk

By road: Buses connect Colombo with Kandy via the main A1 highway, and link Kandy with Nuwara Eliya, Hakgala and Ohiya (for Horton Plains) via the A5. A separate bus route runs southeast on the A8 to connect Colombo and Ratnapura. There are also buses between Ratnapura and Matara, on the south coast. Heading north, express buses connect Kandy with Anuradhapura.

Getting Around

Given the small size of all the hill country towns, including Kandy, the best way of exploring each town is on foot. Other options include three-wheelers and taxis. As usual, agree the fare before setting off. Local buses offer a cheaper way of getting to outlying temples and other sights.

Where to Stay

The few luxury hotels in the hill country are in Kandy and Nuwara Eliya, but there are comfortable mid-range hotels and affordable budget guesthouses throughout the region.

Kandy
Luxury

Amaya Hills Hotel, Heerasgalla, Kandy, tel: 081 447 4022, www.amayahills.com The Kandy area's newest and most luxurious hotel, just outside town, in landscaped grounds.

Mahaweli Reach Hotel, 35 PBA Weerakoon Mawatha, PO Box 78, Kandy, tel: 081 447 2727, www.mahaweli.com The most luxurious place to stay in the region. Outdoor pool, tennis courts, billiard room, and in-room facilities.

The Kandy House, Amunugama Walauwa, Gunnepane, Kandy, tel: 081 492 1394, www.thekandyhouse.com Gorgeous boutique hotel; acclaimed worldwide as the best place to stay in Kandy.

Mid-range

Helga's Folly, 70 Frederick E. Silva Mawatha, tel: 081 223 4571, fax: 081 447 9370, www.helgasfolly.com This family mansion is now an eclectic boutique hotel.

Hotel Tree of Life, Yahalatenna, Werallagama, Kandy, tel: 081 249 9777, fax: 081 249 9711, www.hoteltreeoflife.com Comfortable hotel offering Ayurvedic health treatments, massage, herbal saunas and aromatherapy.

Villa Rosa, 7/18 Dodanwela Passage, Asgiriya, Kandy, tel: 081 221 5556, www.villarosa-kandy.com Hilltop villa guesthouse with lovely river views, on the outskirts of Kandy.

Pinnawala
Budget

Green Land Guest House, Elephant Bath Road, Pinnawala, tel: 035 226 5668, www.greenlandguesthouse.blogspot.com From your balcony at this cosy, budget hotel you can watch the young elephants stroll down for their twice daily bath. It offers air conditioning and internet access and a range of tours and excursions.

Nuwara Eliya
Luxury

Ceylon Tea Trails, Dickoya, tel: 081 774 5700, www.teatrails.com A small collection of luxurious bungalows built for tea plantation managers.

Grand Hotel, Grand Hotel Road, Nuwara Eliya, tel: 052 222 2881, fax: 052 222 2264–5, www.tangerinehotels.com Nuwara Eliya's poshest hotel, next to the golf course. With its billiard room and bars, it reeks of the jolly old British Empire.

Ratnapura
Budget
Rathnaloka Tour Inns, Kosgala, Kahangama, Ratnapura, tel: 045 222 2455, www.rathnaloka.com Reasonable value for money; the only place to stay in Ratnapura!

WHERE TO EAT
Kandy
Mid-range
History Restaurant, 27 Anagarika Dharmapala. Multicultural Asian and Mediterranean dining with a Sri Lankan flavour and surroundings which aim to evoke Kandy's heritage.
The Pub, 36 Dalada Vidiya, tel: 081 223 4868. Slightly bland bar-restaurant with an international menu (grills, salads, pizza and pasta predominate) and an outdoor terrace café with a wider range of alcoholic beverages than most spots in Kandy.

Budget
Sri Ram, 87 Colombo Street, tel: 081 567 7281. Colourfully decorated restaurant specializing in Tamil-South Indian vegetarian dishes. Doesn't serve alcohol.

Nuwara Eliya
Mid-range
Milano, 94 New Bazaar St. Despite its name, Milano serves Chinese dishes and Sri Lankan favourites.
Hill Club Restaurant, 29 Grand Hotel Road, tel: 052 222 2653. This post-colonial restaurant is the poshest place to eat in Nuwara Eliya, with an old-fashioned English-style menu, smartly uniformed waiters and a rather quaint insistence on jacket and tie for male diners.

Ratnapura
Budget
The Rest House Restaurant, Rest House Road, tel: 045 222 2299. Despite its somewhat functional air, this is the best restaurant in Ratnapura, with great views and a menu which offers good vegetarian curries as well as grilled fish and chicken dishes.

TOURS AND EXCURSIONS
Kandy is the gateway to the hill country for travellers from Colombo, and a number of tour companies offer group and individual tailor-made tours around the region's main sights. Tour companies in Colombo (see Colombo At A Glance, p 44–45) also offer a range of itineraries combining the high points of the hill country with the ruined cities and temples of the Cultural Triangle, to the north, and the beaches of the south or west coasts.
JF Tours & Travels, 58 Havelock Road, Colombo 5, tel: 011 258 9402, www.jf tours.com Steam train journeys between Colombo and Kandy aboard the Viceroy Special, as well as tours by rail throughout the country.
A Baur & Co. 5 Upper Chatham Street, Colombo 1, tel: 011 244 8087, fax: 011 244 8493, www.baurs.com This company operates a range of tours including cultural and nature itineraries and bespoke routes.

SHOPPING
Kandy has excellent shopping opportunities. In Nuwara Eliya, there's a smaller range of shops along New Bazaar Street. In Ratnapura (reputed to be the country's gem capital) unmounted gemstones sold in a number of 'gem museums' are not necessarily any cheaper than mounted stones sold in Colombo and Kandy. Gems offered by touts at 'bargain' prices can turn out to be poor-quality stones.

KANDY	J	F	M	A	M	J	J	A	S	O	N	D
AVERAGE TEMP. ºF	57	57	58	60	62	60	60	60	60	60	60	58
AVERAGE TEMP. ºC	14	14	15	16	17	16	16	16	16	16	16	15
RAINFALL in	6.7	1.7	4.3	4.7	6.9	10.9	11.8	7.7	8.9	10.6	9.5	8
RAINFALL mm	170	43	109	119	175	277	300	196	226	269	241	203
DAYS OF RAINFALL	13	6	11	15	18	25	25	22	20	22	22	17

4
Galle and the Southwest

The west coast, south of Colombo, was where Sri Lanka's package holiday industry was born and grew up. Its splendid beaches of fine golden sand continue to attract visitors from all over the world, but there is still some evidence of the catastrophic tsunami which hit the island in 2004. Many of the coastal communities – including the popular resort area of Bentota and the historic town of Galle – were devastated, roads and railway lines were wrecked, and whole villages were destroyed.

Now, however, coconut palms have been replanted, hotels have been restored, and foreign aid has helped to rebuild village schools and clinics. Meanwhile, a new railway line and coastal highway are under construction to connect Colombo, Galle, and the country's huge new seaport and airport at Hambantota.

Sun, sea and sand are the key attractions here, but the region has more to offer than poolside lounging. **Galle**, the regional capital, is steeped in history, with a growing portfolio of 'boutique' hotels and stylish restaurants which offer a welcome alternative to the larger all-inclusive resorts of the **Bentota**, **Hikkaduwa** and **Beruwela** areas. Inland, the **Sinharaja Biosphere Reserve** takes visitors deeper into the unchanged virgin forest. The beach resorts of the southwest can also be easily combined with sightseeing in the hill country or the ancient cities of the 'Cultural Triangle', while Galle has also become a gateway to the rapidly developing south coast.

INDIAN OCEAN

SRI LANKA

Galle

Don't Miss

*** Bentota: Sri Lanka's top hotels, between a fine beach and a lovely river.
*** Hikkaduwa: the country's biggest and liveliest holiday resort beaches, with good coral and diving.
*** Galle: old Dutch town within massive ramparts.
** Sinharaja Biosphere Reserve: a slice of virgin forest sheltering many endemic bird species.

◄ *Opposite: The famous stilt fishermen of Sri Lanka's south coast.*

63

GALLE AND THE SOUTHWEST

▲ *Above: The long stretch of Bentota beach is one of the finest on the island.*

ORUVAS

The **outrigger canoes** called *oruvas* have been used by fishermen off Sri Lanka's shores for more than 2000 years and although they are gradually being replaced by more modern vessels there are still plenty of them around. You'll see them drawn up on beaches everywhere, or beating out to the fishing grounds under sail. Built from local hardwoods with a protective coating of coconut- or shark-liver oil, they can have a working life of up to 30 years.

BERUWALA

Just 60km (38 miles) south of Colombo on the main west coast road, Beruwala is the gateway to the southwest's string of holiday resorts, and many package holiday-makers travel no further than this, perfectly content with its combination of modern hotel accommodation, fine sandy beaches and plenty of bars and restaurants serving inter-national dishes, fine seafood and other Sri Lankan dishes. Tourism, however, has not entirely taken over. Beruwala is home to one of the south's largest fishing fleets and the beach on either side of the Bentota River plays host to the fleet before they set sail for another catch. The river officially separates Beruwala from the adjoining resort strip of Bentota. Just north of the hotel colony, the **Kechimalai Mosque** is built on the spot where the first Muslim traders from the Middle East landed and settled in ad1024. Just south of Beruwela, at Alutgama on the north bank of the Bentota River, there is a colourful and odorous early morning fish market, where outrigger canoes unload their glistening catch.

BENTOTA

Like neighbouring Beruwela, Bentota is dominated by package tourism but the hotels are somewhat newer and more sophisticated. The best stand in splendid isolation on the narrow peninsula between the Bentota River and the sea, with palm-fringed beaches on both the seaward and river sides.

Kosgoda Turtle Hatchery *

About 5km (3 miles) south of Bentota, at the fishing hamlet of Kosgoda, the turtle hatchery releases thousands of hatchlings, mainly green and olive ridley turtles, into the wild. With the help of donations it is currently rebuilding after the tsunami, but welcomes all visitors to view this year's hatchlings (www.kosgodaseaturtle.org).

AMBALANGODA

Ambalangoda, 24km (15 miles) south of Beruwela, is a quiet town which has as yet escaped the attentions of the tourism development industry, though it has a beach to equal those to the north. The main attraction here, is the thriving mask and puppet-making industry, making colourful and grotesque *raksha*, *kolam* and *sanni* masks for Sri Lanka's festivals, processions, and dance-dramas.

Mask Museum **

This private museum and shop is on Ambalangoda's main street 800m (875yd) north of the village centre and is run by one of the village's noted mask-makers. On display are masks symbolizing all the demons, gods, heroes and villains who appear in masked dances and processions. Open daily 09:00–17:00 (www.masksariyapalasl.com).

TURTLES

Bentota's turtle hatcheries are popular tourist attractions where visitors croon over tiny hatchling turtles and pay a small fee to release one into the open sea. The eggs are collected by fishermen and hatched in areas protected from hungry pigs and dogs, but some conservationists now argue this type of hatchery does as much harm as good. Bay turtles normally hatch at night and on reaching the sea swim frantically into deeper, safer waters. If kept in tanks after hatching, then released in daylight, their survival chances may be reduced. Hatcheries are no substitute for protecting the nesting areas used by the turtles for millennia.

▼ *Below: Beruwala is one of the closest beach resorts to the capital.*

GALLE AND THE SOUTHWEST

PERALIYA

One of the most tragic incidents on 26 December 2004 took place when the second giant wave crashed into a stationary train packed with local people travelling down south to visit their family and friends. Over 1000 died. Three of the damaged carriages from the wreck have been transformed into a shrine, a permanent monument where mourners can gather to pray and remember their loved ones.

HIKKADUWA

About 10km (6 miles) to the south of Ambalangoda, Hikkaduwa is the newest and liveliest of the southwest coast beach resorts. Unlike Beruwala and Bentota, it is not completely dominated by large resort hotels, and although it now spreads for some 5km (3 miles) along the coast, its accommodation mix includes small family-run guesthouses as well as larger hotels. There's excellent **snorkelling** just offshore and a number of dive sites for more serious scuba divers further out to sea, while good surf to the south of town attracts surfers.

Coral Gardens ★★★

Even if you're not a scuba diver, Hikkaduwa offers under-

water delights. Only 200m (219yd) offshore, in shallow water no more than 4m (13ft) deep, a reef protects an expanse of brilliant coral populated by the vividly colourful reef fish and even the occasional turtle. It is perfect snorkelling territory. The debris that had accumulated on the reef from the tsunami has now been cleaned away by local divers.

Telwatta Bird Sanctuary ★

Just inland from the main coastal highway, 2km (1.5 miles) south of Hikkaduwa, this small lakeside bird sanctuary offers accessible bird viewing and is especially rich in waterfowl and shorebirds such as the green sandpiper.

GALLE

Galle, located 116km (74 miles) south of Colombo, on the southwest corner of the island, is the largest town in the region. Until the British conquest it was the **most important port** on the island of Sri Lanka, appearing in European histories from as early as AD545.

By the time of the great Arab traveller and writer Ibn Batuta, who landed here in the 13th century, it was firmly established as an entrepôt for commerce between Sri Lanka and the Arab world.

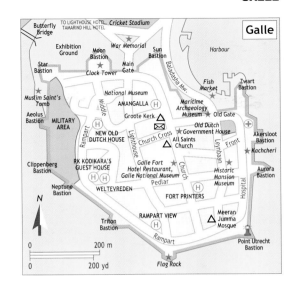

Conquered by the Portuguese in 1505, then by the Dutch in 1640, the town was extensively fortified and the lines of its fortifications — added to by the British through to World War II — can be clearly seen. The tsunami of 2004 damaged the fort's eastern ramparts, mainly the more modern renovations rather than the 17th-century originals, but fortunately much of the interior was spared.

The best-preserved colonial-era city in South Asia, Galle was declared a UNESCO World Heritage Centre in 1988. The city and the surrounding area were hardest hit by the tsunami, but the Dutch colonial buildings within its ring of ramparts have survived in remarkably good shape. Meanwhile, some $57 million has been invested in the reconstruction of hotels, guesthouses, restaurants and other elements of the area's tourism infrastructure, part of a total reconstruction package of US$211 million which has made the charming old town Galle even more attractive than it was before the disaster.

◄ *Opposite: Coconut palms provide shade on all of Sri Lanka's beaches.*

TRADE ROUTES

The Portuguese and Dutch merchantmen who arrived off Sri Lanka's shores in the 16th and 17th centuries were by no means the first western navigators to arrive. The island was known to the Greeks as Taprobane, and appeared on the charts of the mysterious east drawn by the cartographer Ptolemy of Alexandria in the 3rd century BC. Muslim traders from the Gulf called it Serendib, and had established trading depots around the coast centuries before the Portuguese arrived.

▲ Above: The prickly jackfruit is said to be the largest fruit in the world.

The Dutch Fort ★★★

A continuous rampart, built by the Dutch from the mid-17th century onward and added to by the British, encircles the city, interrupted by 14 massive bastions. The best way to see the fort is to walk the length of the walls (90 minutes), and the best time to do it is around sunset. Start at the most impressive section, where the Star, Moon and Sun bastions glower forbiddingly over the neck of the peninsula. The ramparts south of the harbour are pierced by the Old Gate, above which is a British coat of arms (on the inner side, the gate is crowned by the initials of the Dutch East India Company, VOC, and its coat of arms), and south of the harbour the Zwart (Black) Bastion is believed to be the only surviving part of the original Portuguese fortifications. The circuit of the walls continues via the Akersloot and Aurora bastions to the Point Utrecht bastion, topped by a modern lighthouse, then to Flag Rock, the southernmost point of the walls, before looping back north through the Triton, Neptune, Clippenberg and Aeolus bastions. The final section between the Aeolus and Star bastions is closed, as it is part of a military base. While some of the bastions retain their original Dutch names, the Triton, Aeolus, Neptune and Aurora bastions were renamed by the British in honour of the Royal Navy ships of the line which took part in the British seizure of Sri Lanka from the Dutch during the Napoleonic Wars.

Galle National Museum ★

For a peep into life in the days of the Dutch East India Company, look into this small museum at 31 Leynbaan

EARLY TOURISTS

Modern holiday-makers follow in the footsteps of some of the great wanderers of antiquity. The Chinese traveller **Fa-Hsien** visited Anuradhapura in AD412 and wrote an account of the island's wealth – he called it the 'Island of Jewels'. **Marco Polo**, who knew it as 'Serendib', visited it on his way home from China to Venice in 1292, and the Arabic cartographer **Ibn Batuta** visited the Muslim settlement at Galle in 1344. In the 19th century the American author **Mark Twain** was impressed by the island's 'tropical splendours of bloom, of blossom, and Oriental conflagrations of costume!'

Street. Housed in a restored Dutch mansion of the time, it contains paintings, prints, documents, furniture and ceramics from the Dutch colonial era. Open Saturday–Thursday 09:00–17:00 (www.museum.gov.lk).

Groote Kerk (Great Church) ★★

The original 'Great Church', the main church of the Dutch community, was built in 1640. The existing building replaced it in 1755, and its floor contains tombstones from the original cemetery. Open during usual church hours (www.wolvendaal.org).

Maritime Archaeology Museum ★★

Destroyed by the 1994 tsunami, the original National Maritime Museum was reborn in new premises in 2010 with the aid of a Rs177 million grant from the Dutch government. Now housed in the former Dutch East India Company warehouses within the Fort, it displays finds spanning some 800 years of seagoing history, including finds from ancient shipwrecks, maps, cannon and historic craft. Also on display are models of traditional fishing boats and trading vessels from Sri Lanka's south coast. A separate gallery focuses on marine eco-systems such as mangrove tidal zones and coral reefs, and the whale skeleton hanging from the ceiling is a highlight (www.museum.gov.lk).

UNAWATUNA

Unawatuna, less than 5km (3 miles) southward around the coast from Galle, missed out on the tourism boom of the late 20th century

▼ *Below: The Groote Kerk in Galle is a Dutch relic.*

GALLE AND THE SOUTHWEST

because of the troubles. This 4km (2.5-mile) sweep of palm-fringed sand – said by some to be among the twelve best beaches in the world – would no doubt already have gone the way of Beruwala, Bentota and Hikkaduwa.

As it is, Unawatuna, while no longer the well-kept secret of a handful of die-hard backpackers and divers, is still far from over-developed and has bounced back well after the tsunami. Attractions here include sheltered waters for swimming, and an accessible coral reef for snorkelling. For scuba divers, there are several wreck dives only about 20–30 minutes away from the beach by boat.

KOGGALA

Koggala appears in the holiday brochures courtesy of its superb beach, but there is virtually nothing else here except for a handful of all-inclusive resort hotels. That said, it has plenty to recommend it for an idle, undemanding beach holiday.

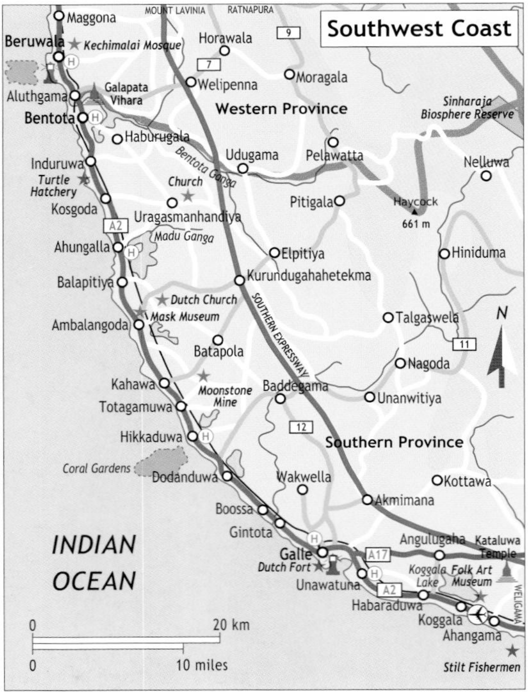

Southwest Coast map

Kataluwa Temple **

At Kataluwa, 2km (1.2 miles) east of Koggala beach, this small Buddhist temple is worth a visit for its frescoes, said to date from the 17th century. The long-nosed, vulpine features in European dress are a less than flattering depiction of the Portuguese merchants who ruled the region at the time.

WELIGAMA

There isn't much to see at

this small fishing port about 30km (20 miles) east of Galle, but the area is known for its **stilt-fishermen**, whose unique style of fishing involves casting their lines from a perch on a sturdy pole 20–50 metres out to sea. Nobody seems to know how or where this unusual technique originated, but it seems to work, as the stilts are passed on from generation to generation and jealously guarded.

SINHARAJA BIOSPHERE RESERVE

This 20km (12-mile) long 'island' of lowland rainforest is 80km (50 miles) northeast of Galle via the A17 highway. It was designated a UNESCO **World Heritage Site** in 1988 and is regarded as one of the most important and bio-diverse conservation areas in Sri Lanka. It has large tracts of un-disturbed forest, but sections thinned by selective logging before the area was declared a reserve make it easy to observe endemic bird species including Sri Lanka spurfowl, Sri Lanka jungle fowl, Sri Lanka wood pigeon, Sri Lanka hanging parrot, Sri Lanka grey hornbill, Sri Lanka mynah and Sri Lanka blue magpie, as well as more than 20 others. Mammal species include the giant squirrel and the endemic purple-faced leaf monkey. Also present, but very rarely seen, are leopard.

To gain access to the reserve, visitors must register and pick up a guide at the Kudawa Forest Department office at the entrance to the camp.

▼ *Below: Relaxing on the beach at Unawatuna, which has not yet become overcrowded.*

BEST TIMES TO VISIT

The southwest coast is most pleasant from September to late April. From May to September, when the monsoon kicks in, the beaches may be pounded by heavy seas and sunshine cannot be guaranteed!

GETTING THERE

By air: At least one luxury hotel resort offers private helicopter transfers (at a price) from Colombo. **Cinnamon Air** (tel: 011 247 5475, www.cinnamonair. com) flies Twin Otter float-planes to and from Bentota and also to the small domestic airport at Koggala from points around Sri Lanka.

By rail: Several services daily between Colombo and Galle, with stops at Alutgama (for Beruwala and Bentota) and Hikkaduwa and onward to Matara. The line will eventually be extended to Kataragama, connecting Galle with the new international airport.

By road: Frequent bus services from Colombo to points all along the southwest coast highway and onward from Galle to Hambantota along the south coast highway. Most luxury and mid-range hotels will arrange private taxi transfers from Colombo International Airport.

GETTING AROUND

Taxis and three-wheelers operate at all resorts, in Galle and other towns. Frequent buses ply the west coast highway, connecting Bentota with Beruwala, Hikkaduwa, Galle and points east.

WHERE TO STAY

Dominated since the 1970s by big package holiday hotels and all-inclusive resorts, the region now also has a growing number of stylish, luxurious and quite expensive boutique hotels, in historic Galle, along the coast and in some lovely inland locations. Budget options are less easy to find.

Bentota
Luxury
Paradise Road: The Villa, 138/18 Galle Road, Bentota, tel: 034 227 5311, www.villabentota.com This is a gorgeous villa-style beachfront hotel comprising 15 designer rooms and suites. The hotel has an acclaimed restaurant.

Mid-range
Vivanta by Taj, National Holiday Resort, Bentota, tel: 034 555 5555, www.vivantabytaj.com Large (162-room) holiday hotel on Bentota's beach, part of the boutique brand of one of Asia's major hotel chains.

Hikkaduwa
Luxury
Aditya, 719/1 Galle Road, Devenigoa, Rathgama, tel: 091 226 7708, www.aditya-resort.com Very charming small luxury hotel with a real sense of style, located on an uncrowded beach but within easy reach of Galle and its shopping and sightseeing.

Mid-range
Asian Jewel Beach Hotel, Baddegawa Road, Nalagasdeniya, Hikkaduwa, tel: 091 493 1388, www.asian-jewel.com Attractive small designer hotel which also offers accommodation in a family-sized, self-catering luxury villa with its own pool.

Sinharaja Biosphere Reserve
Luxury
Boulder Gardens, Sinharaja Road, Koswatta, Kalawana, tel: 045 225 5812/13, www.bouldergardens.com Superbly individual forest hotel, with 10 suites built in and around massive boulders on the fringe of the Sinharaja Biosphere Reserve.

Galle
Luxury
Amangalla, 10 Church Street, Galle, tel: 091 223 3388, www.amanresorts. com The former New Oriental Hotel, now part of

one of the world's finest luxury resort and spa groups, immaculately restored and standing in tropical gardens.

Mid-range
Fort Printers, 39 Pedlar Street, Galle Fort, tel: 091 224 7977, www.thefort printers.com Consists of five suites in an 18th-century house in the heart of historic Galle, with a full-length lap pool in a sheltered courtyard. Surprisingly affordable.
Tamarind Hill, 228 Galle Road, Dadella, tel: 091 222 6568, www. tamarindhill.lk Comfortable, bright and airy rooms surround the colonnaded courtyards of this 19th-century manor house which stands in three acres of its own hilltop grounds.

Koggala
Luxury
The Fortress, Koggala, Galle, tel: 091 438 9400, www.thefortress.lk This gleaming new resort strives to combine old-world colonial charm with the latest leisure, wining and dining facilities.

Unawatuna
Mid-range
Unawatuna Beach Resort, Unawatuna, Galle, tel: 091 438 4545, www.unawatuna beachresort.com Package resort hotel which offers

facilities such as several swimming pools, dive centre and Ayurvedic spa.

WHERE TO EAT
Rebuilding after the havoc wreaked by the 2004 tsunami allowed many of the beach resort hotels to raise their game and improve facilities and menus. Similarly, new upscale restaurants have popped up in the new wave of boutique hotels.

Hikkaduwa
Luxury
Home Grown Rice & Curry Restaurant, tel: 094 724 4078. This tiny, family-run restaurant serves some of the best curries and seafood in Hambantota. Be prepared to wait for a table.

Mid-range
Refresh, 384 Galle Road, Hikkaduwa, tel: 091 227 5783. This restaurant is a long-established favourite with locals and foreign visitors, recommended for its devilled crab and other fresh seafood dishes.

Galle
Luxury
Bamboo Bar and Grill, 18 Upper Dickson Road, tel: 091 438 0275, www.thesun house.com The Sun House's new brasserie is among the best places to eat in Galle, with a menu that blends Sri Lankan, colonial-European

and Southeast Asian influences. Reservations recommended.

Budget
India Hut, Rampart Street, Galle Fort, no telephone. Great value South Indian dishes served on the walls of the old fort.
Seagreen Restaurant, Rampart Street, Galle Fort, tel: 091 224 2754. This restaurant serves tasty and very affordable seafood, and also freshly squeezed juices.

TOURS AND EXCURSIONS
Windsurfing, kite-boarding and other water sports are offered by numerous independent operators on the beaches of Bentota and Beruwala, and can aso be easily arranged through all resort hotels.

Submarine Diving School, Walla Dewala Road, Unawatuna, tel: 077 719 6753, www.divinginsrilanka. com Offers scuba training, snorkelling and dive trips for novices and expert divers.

EcoTeam Sri Lanka (www. srilankaecotourism.com) arranges wildlife and birding trips in the Sinharaja Biosphere Reserve as well as an array of safaris and animal- and bird-spotting journeys throughout the country's national parks and reserves.

5
The South Coast

The south coast, until recently, was a well-kept tourism secret, with only a few independent travellers and cognoscenti travelling east of Galle. But since the tragic impact of the tsunami in 2004, and the end of the civil war, a dramatic transformation has taken place, and continues. Vast amounts of money have been invested in reconstruction and development. A new major highway is under construction, linking Galle, on the island's southwest tip, with **Hambantota**. Here, where the coast begins to curve northward, a once-sleepy fishing village and independent travellers' haven has become a hotbed of development and industrialization. A vast new seaport, intended to become the largest in South Asia, is under construction. A large new international airport opened in 2013, but is so far served only by flights from Colombo, Dubai and Abu Dhabi. Both will eventually be connected to the capital by the new highway and a new stretch of railway from **Matara** in the west to **Kataragama** in the east.

Greater access to the south coast has already spurred hotel development on the superb beaches that are even more attractive than those of the better-known west coast. Lessons seem to have been learned from excesses of large-scale resort development (not just in Sri Lanka but worldwide), and most of the new properties are on a smaller scale than those of Bentota and Negombo. Meanwhile, Sri Lanka's potential as an ecotourism destination is being unleashed as it becomes easier for visitors to reach some of the

DON'T MISS

*** Uda Walawe National Park: sanctuary for many mammal and bird species.
*** Bundala National Park: scrub jungle surrounding large pools attracting birds and marine turtles.
*** Kataragama: Sri Lanka's second most sacred place of pilgrimage.
*** Ruhuna (Yala) National Park: Sri Lanka's largest and most popular national park.

◀ *Opposite: Dondra Head lighthouse stands at the southern tip of Sri Lanka.*

THE SOUTH COAST

country's finest wildlife areas, including the **Udu Walawe National Park** and the massive **Ruhuna (Yala) National Park** and its satellite sanctuaries. The impact of development on the smaller **Bundala National Park** and the **Debarawewa Wetland**, right under the footprint of the new seaport and airport, may be less positive.

Inland, the south coast also has some remarkable temples – not, perhaps as impressive as the great sites of the 'Cultural Triangle', but interesting and emotive in their own way.

▲ *Above: The Star Fort at Matara was built in 1763 to guard the river crossing to the main fort.*

MATARA

Matara was until very recently the largest town on the south coast east of Galle. Centuries ago, it was an important *entrepôt* for the spice and gem trade with the Arab world, and

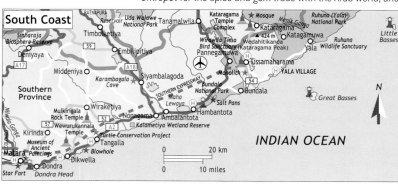

it was also a strategic asset for the Dutch. Separated from the mainland by the Nilwala Ganga estuary, the oldest part of town stands within the defensive walls that they built in the mid-17th century. The damage wrought by the 2004 tsunami here is still evident. Restoration of the surviving colonial buildings continues, but Matara's future as a work aday town or a tourist hub seems uncertain. It has lost its status as the key port and railhead on the south coast to the burgeoning new seaport and airport hub at Hambantota. A new coast highway and railway have made it much easier for travellers to bypass Matara in favour of points east.

Star Fort and Museum of Ancient Paintings *
An outpost of the Dutch fortifications on the north bank of the Nilwala Ganga, about 350m (360yd) from the main gate, this small, five-pointed stronghold was built in 1763 to guard the river crossing. Within, a small museum is dedicated to the visual arts of the ancient Sinhalese kingdoms, with authentic copies of mural paintings and drawings and the tools and pigments used to make them. Open Wed—Mon 08:30—17:00, closed Tuesday.

Dondra Head (Dewi Nuwara) *
Built by the British in 1889, this octagonal lighthouse marks the southernmost tip of Sri Lanka. It stands just over 1km (640yd) south of Dondra village, on the main coast highway, 6km (4 miles) east of Matara.

DIKWELLA **
Dikwella, about 24km (15 miles) east of Matara, is, like other south coast villages, still recovering from the impact of the 2004 tsunami, which devastated its handful of beachside guesthouses and small restaurants. However, its long sandy beach is still spectacular, mass tourism has yet to arrive in force, and following rebuilding efforts accommodation now ranges from a few classy hotels to smaller guesthouses. Dikwella is renowned as a centre for the so called '**Devil Dance**', whose masked performers are credited with the

---

WHALE-WATCHING

In May 2008 Jetwing Eco Holidays (www.jetwingeco.com) publicized the work they had done with marine biologist Charles Anderson and Mirissa Water Sports. In the period between December to April, with peaks in December and April, the seas south of Dondra is one of the best locations in the world for Blue whales and Sperm whales.

THE SOUTH COAST

INCARNATIONS OF THE BUDDHA

Before being born into a Hindu royal family, the Buddha had several previous incarnations, during each of which, through right conduct, he gained the moral strength to reach enlightenment as a man. The Jataka folk tales of the Buddha's life, which are illustrated in frescoes in many of Sri Lanka's temples, tell how the Buddha was born as a six-tusked white elephant, as a monkey and as a golden stag before his final incarnation as Prince Siddartha, son of King Suddhodana of Kapilavastu, in what is now Nepal.

power to drive out evil spirits and help the sick to recover. The area is also famous for the lace-making skills of local women, whose work can be seen and bought at the **Dikwella Lace Cooperative**, where young women are trained in the traditional craft.

'Hummanya' Blowhole *

On the coast at Kudawela, 6km (4 miles) east of Dikwella, this natural phemonenon attracts a steady flow of sightseers. Ocean wave pressure forces water up through a narrow fissure, causing a surge of foam and spray that shoots up to 40m (120ft) into the air. This happens about four times an hour, and is at its most impressive during June and July.

Wewurukannala Temple **

Sri Lankan Buddhists claim that the 50m (160ft) Buddha image within the courtyard of this modern temple complex is the tallest in the world. Around it, hundreds of garish, life-size effigies act out scenes from the life of the Buddha and warn of the demonic afterlife that awaits those who sin against Buddhist doctrine. Rebuilt in 1966 on the site

of a temple complex dating from the late 18th century, it has none of the sense of awe that surrounds Buddhism's more ancient shrines. For a donation to temple funds, you can climb up the enclosed stair behind the colossal statue for a panoramic Buddha's-eye view. Open daily, dawn until dusk, admission by donation.

◀ Left: Tangalla is great for a beach holiday.
◀ Opposite: A giant Buddha image at Wewurukannala stands among hundreds of life-size statues acting out scenes from Buddhist myth and legend.

Tangalla ★★★

Tangalla (also known as Tangalle) suffered terribly when it was hit by the 2004 tsunami, which killed thousands of local people, destroyed their homes and livelihoods, and washed away almost all the small guesthouses and restaurants along the long beach north of the village and the sandy coves to the south.

Since then, the community has become the focus of a low-scale yet up-market resort area where a number of chic boutique hotels have appeared where previously only the most basic of guesthouses existed. Tangalla's renaissance is unsurprising. Just 48km (30 miles) east of Matara, it was only a matter of time before this idyllic spot roughly midway along the south coast was discovered. Nevertheless, Tangalla is still a long way from over-development, and is one of the most pleasant places in Sri Lanka for a lazy beach holiday. The core of the village faces east, straddling a freshwater lagoon and a fishing harbour at the mouth of a small river. To the north, **Medaketiya** beach – the best and sandiest in the region – keeps its relaxed feel, and the local

> ## WHAT TO WEAR
>
> Sri Lankans of all groups are generally modest and find displays of too much skin embarrassing and offensive. Beachwear should only be worn at beach resorts. Away from the beach, cotton garments are best. In the hill country you may want a long-sleeved shirt or wrap after dark when it gets a little cooler.

THE SOUTH COAST

▲ *Above: Spotted deer in Uda Walawe National Park.*

turtle conservation projects endeavour to preserve stretches of beach so that sea turtles can continue to breed here.

Mulkirigala Rock Temple *

At Mulkirigala, 16km (10 miles) north of Tangalla, this cave temple in a monolithic rock contains reclining Buddha figures in smiling repose as well as standing and seated Buddha figures, surrounded by wall paintings depicting scenes from the life of the Buddha. The rock is crowned by a **Buddhist shrine**. Open daily during daylight hours.

Rekawa Turtle Conservation Project **

This patch of beach about 8km (5 miles) east of Tangalle is the hub of the turtle conservation efforts on the south coast and has a visitor centre and a programme of guided visits. Each night between January and July up to 30 green turtles lay their eggs here, along with four other marine turtle species. Project workers move eggs from unprotected nests to sites that are protected against animal and human predators (www.turtlewatchrekawa.org).

Kalametiya **

About 32km (20 miles) east of Tangalla, off the A2 coast highway at the 218km (135-mile) marker, the future of this wetland refuge for migrating waterfowl and waders is doubtful. The tsunami destroyed the sandbar which separated the lagoon from the open sea, with radical changes to its ecosystem. Construction of the huge new Hambantota seaport and the concomitant increase in marine traffic in nearby waters may also have an impact. Studies continue. In the meantime, visitors can hope to see several migrant birds including four species of plover, curlew, marsh sandpiper, curlew sandpiper, greenshank and yellow wagtail. Residents include three kinds of egret, spoonbill, glossy ibis, purple swamphen and black-winged stilt.

UDA WALAWE NATIONAL PARK

This 30,821ha (76,159-acre) national park offers an accessible slice of Sri Lankan wilderness, providing a refuge for elephants, toque money, grey langur, spotted deer, wild pig, leopard and sambur, as well as more than 100 bird species, including white-bellied sea eagle, crested serpent eagle, and changeable hawk eagle. The park surrounds a large artificial lake, the **Uda Walawe Reservoir**, fed by the Walawe Ganga, the river which then flows south to meet the sea at Ambalantota. Created in 1972 from abandoned plantations, open grassland and scrub jungle, Uda Walawe is easy to reach — only 100km (64 miles) north of Hambantota and about the same distance south of Ratnapura, off the A18 highway. This accessibility creates some problems: illegal settlements and grazing on the edge of the park, occasional poaching, and an ever-increasing number of visitors in their own vehicles. Urban development and the post-tsunami growth of tourism on the south coast may add to these problems.

POYA DAYS

Poya (worship) days fall on **each full moon** and each is a public holiday, when people travel all over Sri Lanka to worship at local shrines and visit family and friends. Finding bus and train seats becomes difficult, and no alcohol is on sale (some restaurants and bars will sell drinks discreetly to foreigners, though not to Sri Lankans). Starting with *Duruthu Poya* (which is held to coincide with New Year's Day) the *poya* calendar is as follows:
Duruthu Poya
Navam Poya
Medin Poya
Bak Poya
Adhi Vesak Poya
Vesak Poya / and the day following *Vesak Poya*
Poson Poya
Esala Poya
Nikini Poya
Binara Poya
Vap Poya
Il Poya
Unduwap Poya

◀ *Left: Painted storks are among the many spectacular birds at Uda Walawe.*

THE SOUTH COAST

HAMBANTOTA

The troubles of the 1980s and 1990s, plus the difficulty of getting here from Colombo (a 240km journey) kept the brakes on tourism development around this uninspiring provincial town for years, although nearby beaches attracted a trickle of independent travellers.

Then the area was devastated by the 2004 tsunami, and reconstruction took an unexpected turn. Instead of being redeveloped as a fully fledged resort, Hambantota is in the process of becoming the largest **commercial seaport** in South Asia, with port facilities stretching along a 16km (10-mile) expanse of coastline. A large new international airport opened nearby in 2013.

In the process, Hambantota's population is expected to grow from approximately 10,000 to more than 50,000, drawing in people from tsunami-hit communities and inland villages in search of relatively high-paying work.

There are also concerns about the inevitable impact on nearby national parks and nature reserves, including the **Hambantota Salt Pans** (just east of Hambantota), the Lewala wetlands of the **Bundala National Park**, and the coastline of the Ruhuna Wildlife Sanctuary. To balance this,

▶ *Right: Outrigger canoes pulled up out of reach of the surf at Hambantota beach.*

easier access to one of the country's largest reserves, the **Ruhunu National Park** and its satellite areas, will (if properly managed) be likely to boost Sri Lanka as an **ecotourism** destination and increase awareness of its wildlife areas as a tourism resource.

Bundala National Park ★★★

About 16km (10 miles) east of Hambantota, Bundala is an accessible expanse of scrub jungle surrounding large shallow pools which attract many bird species. The beaches are egg-laying sites for Olive Ridley and leather-back **turtles**. Hawksbill and green turtles are less frequently seen. Other large reptiles include water monitors and crocodiles, and among the mammal species to be seen within the park boundaries are elephant, spotted deer, grey langur and jackal.

Bundala is a relatively small park (compared with the huge expanse of Yala/Ruhuna to the east) but its high concentrations of **mammal** and **bird species** make it one of the best places to see Sri Lanka's abundant wildlife. It is open all year round, unlike Yala/Ruhuna – closed in August– October. Bundala has remained vibrant since the tsunami with good levels of bird and animal life. The water had minimal impact on the park. Beach erosion is thought to naturally rectify itself within two years, and breaches of the sand dunes have already been replaced. Though, over 75 nests were lost at the time, turtles are returning to nest in good numbers.

Diving ★★

The **Great Basses** reef, about 40km (25 miles) east of Hambantota, and the **Little Basses**, 80km (50 miles) east, are reputed to offer the best diving in Sri Lanka, with numerous wrecks and many large pelagic fish species to be seen. Both islands are uninhabited and characterized by lighthouses built in the mid-19th century to point out these hazards to shipping. Very strong currents mean these dive sites are suitable only for experienced divers.

THE MALDIVES

Many tour operators offer holidays which combine a tour of Sri Lanka with a stay on one of the hundreds of coral atolls of the Maldives, the **independent island republic** some 720km (450 miles) southwest of Sri Lanka or one hour's flying time from Colombo. Tourism develop-ment has been permitted only on uninhabited atolls to reduce its impact on island society, and there are several luxurious resort islands with comfortable village-style accommodation, superb white sand beaches and excellent scuba diving.

MONSOONS

The annual monsoon winds, bringing **heavy rain** and **pound-ing surf** to Sri Lanka's shores, are caused by temperature and air pressure differentials between the Indian Ocean and the Asian landmass, with prevail-ing winds sucking humid air off the ocean in summer to cause the southwest monsoon rains. In winter the prevailing winds shift, and cooler, drier air creates the northeast monsoon, with rains that are not usually as heavy as the southwest monsoon.

▲ *Above: Snorkelling is a popular activity on Sri Lanka's south coast.*

TISSAMAHARAMA

Tissamaharama ('Tissa' for short) has so far owed its steady trickle of visitors to its handy location close to Ruhunu National Park. About 40km (25 miles) northeast of Hambantota, it is also close to the new international airport – a factor which is already changing the face of this once-sleepy community. The town centre is embellished by an enormous tank (reservoir), the **Tissa Wewa**, built some 2300 years ago by Yatalatissa, founder of the ancient kingdom of Ruhuna, whose capital was here. His heir, **Kanatissa**, endowed the two large dagobas which stand nearby.

KATARAGAMA

Kataragama, located about 80km (50 miles) northeast of Hambantota, is second only to Adam's Peak as a place of pilgrimage, attracting Sri Lankan Muslims, Buddhists and Hindus during the July–August pilgrimage and festival season. Kataragama's highest-profile event is the slightly grisly **Thaipusam** fire-walking festival (*see* panel, page 85).

Like nearby Tissa, Kataragama is close to the new international airport and will also become the terminus of a new highway and a new railway linking the south coast with Galle and Colombo and the impact of this increased accessibility is likely to be quite dramatic.

Sacred Precinct ★★

North of the small modern town, the Sacred Precinct comprises Buddhist, Tamil Hindu and Muslim places of worship. The main entrance is at the corner of Saddhatissa Mawatha and Sellakataragama Road, from which a bridge crosses the **Menik Ganga** ('Jewel River') which flows through the site. At the north end of the bridge stands the **Shiva Kovil**, a Hindu temple; just north of it is the Muslim **ul-Khizr Mosque**, while about 300m to the northwest stands the unprepossessing **Maha Devale** temple, which is said to contain the spear of the 12-armed Hindu-Buddhist warrior god **Skanda**, who is also known here as Kataragama.

Other Hindu gods represented here include **Vishnu**, one of the three supreme Hindu deities, and elephant-headed **Ganesha**, god of prosperity and success.

The temple complex is very old; the earliest shrine to the resident god is credited to a 2nd-century-BC local ruler, **Dutugemunu**, and the most important Buddhist shrine, the **Kirivehera Dagoba**, was erected in the 1st century BC. A recently built museum, next to the Maha Devale, contains fragments of statuary from several of the shrines and other nearby temples.

▼ *Below: Fire-walking: a case of calloused feet or deep religious faith?*

THE SOUTH COAST

COCONUTS

The coconut palms which line Sri Lanka's beaches and cover much of the lowlands are more than just decorative. Coconut products account for **2 per cent** of **Sri Lanka's exports**, in the form of dried coconut meat and coir, the tough fibre made from the husk of the coconut. Discarded shells are used as fuel, and beach hawkers make a living selling freshly plucked orange-coloured coconuts, a popular thirst quencher, to sunbathers on the beach at Bentota or Hikkaduwa.

Thaipusam Festival ★★★

Like some other Tamil Hindu religious events throughout Asia, the annual festival known as Thaipusam — when pilgrims converge on the site from all over Sri Lanka, many of them making the pilgrimage on foot through the hills from Batticaloa on the east coast — seems to have a strong masochistic streak. Devout celebrants allow metal skewers to be driven through their cheeks and tongues, or haul heavy carts carrying symbols and images of the temple deities by cables attached to their backs and shoulders by steel hooks. Gory though it appears, it is well attested that the wounds caused by skewers and hooks bleed little — perhaps because large amounts of adrenaline are produced by the body — and heal very quickly. **Fire-walking**, when devotees walk across a bed of glowing coals, is another apparently painful activity from which participants seem to emerge unscathed.

Open all the time; and during *puja* (daily worship) at Maha Devala, at 04:30, 10:30, 18:30. The Kataragama Thaipusam Festival takes place annually over two weeks in July and August; dates can be obtained from Sri Lanka Tourism information offices in Colombo and overseas (*see* Travel Tips, page 122).

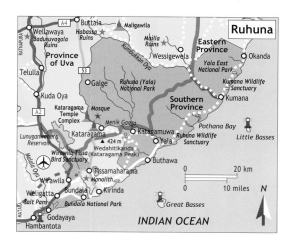

RUHUNA NATIONAL PARK (YALA)

Ruhuna is the most accessible of the five blocks which comprise the Yala National Park and one of only two which are open to the public. It is easily reached from Colombo or the A2 coastal highway, the park entrance is approximately 70km (45 miles) east of Hambantota and 30km (19 miles) east of Tissa.

Ruhuna covers almost

RUHUNA NATIONAL PARK (YALA)

1000km² (386 sq miles) of scrub jungle, open savannah, riverine woodland and a long coastline which curves around Sri Lanka's southeast coast. However, only the southwest segment of the park, an area of some 130km² (50 sq miles), is open to visitors. Ruhuna is the best park in Sri Lanka for spotting **mammals**. However, this is not Africa – the terrain makes animals harder to spot, and there isn't the density of grazers you would see in parks of East or southern Africa. Asian forests have mammals in lower numbers but are still rich in species. Yala does have a very high density of leopards because of good numbers of spotted deer being present (www.yalasrilanka.lk).

Touring the Park

Leopards and **elephants** get top billing and are what most people come to see, to the extent that joy-riding visitors in jeeps are increasingly driving the animals out of the visitable sector of the park and into its less accessible areas. Other mammals include sloth bear, spotted deer, mouse deer, barking deer, sambur, grey langur, toque monkey, wild boar, and smaller species including stripe-necked and ruddy mongoose and jackal. Both marsh and estuarine crocodiles may be seen, and a day's birding can record as many as 100 species, among them such rarities as red-faced malkoha, great thickknee, sirkeer malkoha, blue-faced malkoha and painted stork.

Access is by vehicle only, and **four-wheel drive** would be useful. Ruhuna is usually closed from late August to mid-October. The best time to be sure of seeing the maximum is during the dry season, when animals cluster around water sources in multi-species groups. Though the coastal strip of the park suffered during the inundation, very few animals perished prompting scientists to wonder whether the fauna species sensed the impending disaster in some way unknown to humans.

▼ Below: Elephants can be seen in large numbers in Ruhuna National Park.

THE SOUTH COAST AT A GLANCE

BEST TIMES TO VISIT
September to late April is the best time to visit the south coast. The **monsoon season** affects this area from May to September, making the seas rough and reducing the chances of sunshine.

GETTING THERE
By air: A large new airport has opened at Hambantota, with flights by airlines including Sri Lanka Airlines, Mihin Lanka (www.mihin lanka.com) and Rotana Jet (www.rotanajet.com) from Colombo and a number of other points in Asia and the Middle East.

By road: A new highway is under construction between Galle and Kataragama, detouring inland via the new airport. Buses connect Colombo with Hambantota via Galle and Matara (journey time 4–6 hours). Buses also operate from Hambantota to Colombo via Ratnapura, and Kandy via Nuwara Eliya.

By rail: A new railway line connecting Colombo and Galle with Hambantota and Kataragama, originally intended for completion in 2011, was scheduled to open in 2015.

GETTING AROUND
There are three-wheelers and taxis in Hambantota and other main villages such as Dikwella, Tangalla and Tissamaharama. At Matara, bullock-drawn carriages with lumpy red upholstery are still an everyday form of public transport, and rather a novelty for any tourist! Moving at no more than walking pace, they are a great way to tour around the old town. The best option is a three-wheeler or a taxi, readily available in the main villages. Matara has an interesting option: bullock-drawn carriages with red upholstery.

GETTING AROUND THE PARKS
All the parks are accessible independently by renting a 4WD vehicle and driver. For **Uda Walawe National Park**, 4WD vehicles with driver can be hired at the Centauria Tourest Hotel (*see* Where to Stay). For **Ruhuna** and **Bundala** national parks, almost 200 drivers tout for business at the south end of Kataragama Road (beside the Tissa Wewa lake). However, for all the parks, travelling with a specialist wildlife tour company (*see* Tours and Excursions) generally offers a much better experience.

WHERE TO STAY
The 2004 tsunami wiped out many of the south coast's small seafront guesthouses. Extensive rebuilding has produced boutique hotels, low-rise resorts and rebuilt guesthouses, with Tangalle emerging as the south coast's hub for chic (and expensive) accommodation.

Matara
Mid-range
Sanaya Mansion, 200 Galle Road, Pambarana, Matara, tel: 041 223 3221, www.sanaya-mansion-matara-sri.lanka.lakpura.com Comfortable modern hotel with pool and restaurant, more than adequate for an overnight stop.

Budget
Beach Inns, tel: 041 222 6356, www.beach-inns.com Small family-run guest house on a quiet stretch of beach.

Tangalle
Luxury
Amanwella, Godellawela, Goyambokka, tel: 047 224 1333, www.amanresorts.com Stupendous (and costly) luxury low-rise resort that sets the benchmark for stylish, upscale accommo-dation on the south coast.

Turtle Bay, Kalamatiya, Tangalle, tel: 094 4477 887 853, www.turtlebay.lk This charming boutique hotel has tranquil rooms and offers yoga and other therapeutic activities.

Mid-range
Mangrove Beach Cabanas, Marakolliya, Kapuhenwella, Tangalle, www.beach cabana.lk Thatched wooden cabanas, family-sized chalets and mud-brick houses among palms on the sandy beach, with its own restaurant and bar. Super value for money.

Dikwella
Luxury
Dickwella Beach Resort, tel: 041 225 5271, www.lolcleisure.com One of the first luxury hotels to open in the area (in 1975), still very much one of the pleasantest after a thorough renovation.

Mid-range
Manahara Beach Cabanas, Mahawela Road, Moraktiyara, Nakulagamuwa, tel: 047 224 0585, www.manaharabeachcabanas.com This complex of red-tiled miniature cottages and split-level villas on the beach is within walking distance of the famous 'blowhole' and has a good seafood restaurant.
Tallala Retreat, Sampaya House, Tallala South, Gandara, tel: 041 225 9171, www.tallalaretreat.com Very attractive complex with villa-style accommodation in tropical gardens on a superb stretch of beach, offering activities such as yoga, surfing classes and snorkelling.

National Parks
Uda Walawe National Park
Mid-range
Centauria Tourest Hotel, New Town, Embelipitiya, tel: 047 223 0514, www.centauriahotel.com This lakeside hotel offers the most comfortable accommodation within easy reach of Uda Walawe and also arranges tours in the park.

Ruhuna
Luxury
Yala Village Hotel, Yala (10km from Kirinda, 22km south of Tissa), tel: 047 223 9450, www.srilankayala.com On the fringes of the park, with an observation deck from which elephants and even leopard may sometimes be seen, beside a long stretch of beach and set in 10 acres of jungle and parkland, this chalet complex is the most luxurious accommodation in the Yala/Ruhuna area.

WHERE TO EAT
Many of the small beach-side restaurants and food shacks in places along the south coast were swept away by the tsunami, and have not yet all been rebuilt. That said, basic restaurants serving curries and other local favourites, grilled seafood and rice and noodle dishes can be found everywhere, and there are plenty of roadside food stalls next to markets, bus stations and harbours. For somewhat more up-market dining, each of the hotels and guesthouses listed under Where to Stay has at least one good restaurant.

TOURS AND EXCURSIONS
Trips to the national parks of the south with your own four-wheel-drive vehicle and driver can easily be organized on the spot in Hambantota or Tissamaharama, where local drivers actively tout for business at the bus stations and guesthouses. Most hotels and guesthouses will help to arrange vehicles and drivers, and also provide meals to take with you. Cost is a matter for negotiation and you should make a firm agreement on the price before leaving, specifying exactly what you will and won't pay for. Visits to the parks of the south can be arranged through several companies, including:
Kulu Safaris, 6 Horathapola Estate, Wadumunnegedara, tel: 037 493 1662, www.kulusafaris.com Safari-style tours, accommodation in mobile tented camps at selected locations in Yala, Wilpattu and Uda Walawe, and escorted wildlife and birding tours in the south and the rest of the country.
Sri Lanka Ecotourism, 20/43 Fairfield Gardens, Colombo 8, tel: 011 583 0833, www.srilankaecotourism.com All kinds of escorted wildlife and activity tours.
A Baur & Co, Wildlife and Birdwatching Service, 5 Upper Chatham Street, Colombo 1, tel: 011 244 8087, fax: 011 244 8493, www.baurs.com
Whalewatching Mirissa, Hill Side, Mirissa, tel: 094 71 312 1061, www.whalewatchingmirissa.com Whale and dolphin watching cruises and river trips.

6
Anuradhapura and the Northwest

The ancient heritage attractions of Sri Lanka's '**Cultural Triangle**' complement the beach resorts of the south and west coast, while the rolling, open fields and artificially irrigated rice fields of the northwest 'dry zone' provide an interesting contrast with the cool, lush tea country of the central hill country.

The region is dominated by ancient temples and fortresses such as **Sigiriya**, crowning rocky pinnacles above dusty plains, and the remnants of ancient royal capitals such as **Anuradhapura** and **Polonnaruwa**. Huge rock-cut Buddha images, dagobas and cave temples testify to an ancient Buddhist tradition.

The hub of the Cultural Triangle is Anuradhapura, founded in 475BC by the Sinhala King Pandukhabaya. For more than 1000 years, this was the capital of an empire that was famed throughout Asia. It was also the place from which Buddhist beliefs spread to Sri Lanka, after the Murya Emperor of India, Ashok, sent envoys who persuaded King Devanampiya Tissa (247–207BC) to adopt Buddhism.

As well as these ancient sites, this part of the island also has some fine and (so far) undeveloped beaches, scuba diving, and Sri Lanka's largest national park, **Wilpattu**.

Until 2010, the security situation made travel to the northern sectors of Wilpattu and north of Anuradhapura problematic. Travellers may still encounter military checkpoints when travelling by road into the Vavuniya and Mannar districts, north of Anuradhapura.

DON'T MISS

*** Anuradhapura: ruined capital of Sri Lanka's greatest kingdom, rediscovered in the 19th century.
*** Polonnaruwa: thousand-year-old ruined imperial city.
*** Sigiriya: dizzy cliff-top citadel with superb views and 1700-year-old rock paintings.
** Dambulla: cliffside cave temple with dozens of Buddha images.

◀ *Opposite: The reclining and standing rock-carved Buddhas at the Gal Vihara.*

▲ *Above: The quadrangle complex at Anuradhapura encloses a rich collection of ancient buildings.*

In January/February 2011, parts of the region, including **Dambulla** and **Sigiriya**, were hit by severe **flooding** which affected road access and damaged some ancient sites as well as tourist hotels. The floods, of course, also damaged local infrastructure such as schools and hospitals, and cost a number of lives.

DAMBULLA

For the visitor heading into the Cultural Triangle from the south, Dambulla (72km/45 miles north of Kandy) is the first stop on the way. The finest and most famous of Sri Lanka's Buddhist **cave temples** stands 150m (162yd) outside modern Dambulla; within five large caverns are dozens of centuries-old sitting, standing and reclining Buddha images and Hindu deities. Each cave is also adorned with scenes from the Buddha's life. The temples were reputedly created by Valagam Bahu (104–76BC), King of Anuradhapura, who

HABARANA

Although it is of no great interest in itself, the small town of Habarana is the most **convenient base** for exploring Dambulla and Sigiriya, with a choice of mid-range and budget accommodation and a handful of simple restaurants.

took refuge here after being driven from his throne by South Indian invaders. The caves are on the higher part of one of the smooth rock outcrops which are a feature of the regional landscape, and the ascent is steep; while this edition was researched, access had been affected by flooding. Normal opening times: daily 06:00–19:00 (www.goldentemple.lk).

SIGIRIYA

This 200m (656ft) basalt plug was fortified around AD473–480 by Kasyapa, a prince of Anuradhapura who had killed his father and usurped the throne from his brother Mogallana, the rightful heir.

Mogallana defeated his brother in AD491, Kasyapa committed suicide, and Mogallana was crowned king in AD495. He returned the throne to Anuradhapura and reigned until AD513. Sigiriya was abandoned, and its treasures were not rediscovered by European colonialists until the 19th century.

Palace Complex ★★★

Below the crag, the ramparts of the lower citadel enclose a complex of ruined miniature palaces and swimming pools.

In Kasyapa's time, the rock wall of the stair was graced by hundreds of paintings of skimpily clad beauties. Only 22 of these **Sigiriya Damsels** remain – the only secular art surviving from that era. Nearby, the **Mirror Wall** is covered with graffiti dating from as early as the 8th century AD, providing linguists with useful insight into the evolution of the Sinhala language. The final section of the stair entered the upper citadel

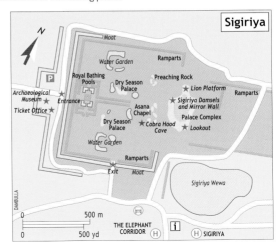

Sigiriya

ANURADHAPURA AND THE NORTHWEST

▶ *Right: The Sigiriya rock fortress rises high above the flat plains of the dry zone.*

SRI LANKAN BIRDS

Among the most colourful of Sri Lanka's **33 endemic bird species** is the blue magpie, with its vivid turquoise chest and back, white-barred blue tail, chestnut head and red eye and beak. Equally striking is the red-faced malkoha, with its glossy black back, wings and tail, white front, bare red pate and greenish, curved beak. The Sri Lanka jungle fowl closely resembles a domestic cockerel, with russet plumage, green-black tail feathers and a red comb and wattle. An unusual species is the Sri Lankan hanging parrot, with a red cap, yellow nape and bright green wings and breast. The name hanging parrot comes from their unusual habit of sleeping upside down.

between the paws of a colossal brickwork lion, hence its name, meaning 'lion rock'. All that remains of Kasyapa's lofty palace is his stone throne and a reservoir carved from the rock, but the view is breathtaking.

The **Sigiriya Museum** (admission included with site ticket, same opening hours) traces the history of settlement on and around the rock from around 8000BC to the height of King Kasyapa's 'golden age' (www.ccf.lk/sigiriya).

POLONNARUWA

Built more than 1000 years ago, Polonnaruwa is the better preserved of the two ancient capitals of the northwest. The ruins are just north of modern Polonnaruwa, 140km (90 miles) north of Kandy.

POLONNARUWA

Ancient City ★★★

Polonnaruwa was built in the late 10th century AD after the conquest of Anuradhapura by the Chola dynasty, from southern India. The Cholas built their new capital as a bulwark against the unconquered Sinhala kingdom of Ruhuna, but in 1070 they were driven out by the Sinhalese ruler Vijayabahu I, who strengthened its defences and added huge temples, palaces, tanks (reservoirs) and gardens. The Sinhalese were driven back in the 13th century by new invasions from India, and Polonnaruwa fell into disuse.

The most impressive surviving buildings date from the reign of King Parakramabahu I (1153–86), Polonnaruwa's

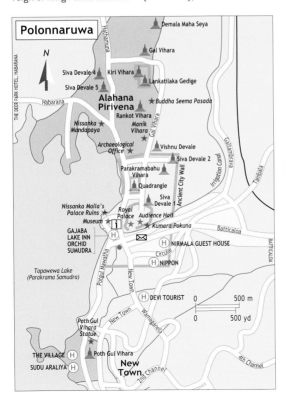

THE LION KING

The semi-legendary **King Vijaya** (543–505BC) is regarded by the Sinhalese as the first king of Sri Lanka and the **forefather** of their race. Vijaya was said to be descended from a princess of the Kalinga kingdom of Bengal, who mated with a lion to produce a twin son and daughter, Sinhabahu and Sinhabvali, from whose marriage Vijaya was born. Exiled from his father's kingdom, Vijaya reached Sri Lanka, where he married first a demon princess, Kuveni, then a human princess from southern India, and founded the line of Sinhalese kings.

KASYAPA AND DHATUSENA

When Kasyapa, the builder of Sigiriya, ousted his father King Dhatusena from the throne, he tortured him to discover where his treasure was concealed. Before his execution, Dhatusena asked to be allowed to bathe one final time in the tank he had built at Kalawewa. Taking a handful of the water, he said: 'This is all the treasure I have'. The furious Kasyapa had him chained and walled up alive to die of thirst. The tale surely symbolizes the importance of water and irrigation systems to the empires of Anuradhapura and Polonnaruwa.

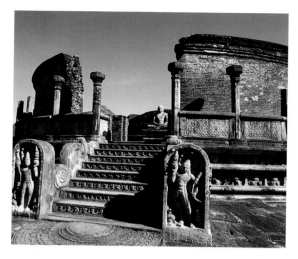

▲ *Above: Audience Hall of the Royal Palace, where kings of Polonnaruwa met emissaries of other nations.*
▶ *Opposite: The Vatadage at Polonnaruwa houses four Buddha images.*

heyday. Within the walls, on the east shore of the artificial Topa Wewa Lake, stand dozens of shrines and palaces.

Polonnaruwa Visitor Information Centre and Museum ★★★

The visitor centre uses a five-minute video presentation, designer displays, a collection of archaeological finds (including a wonderful frieze of dwarf figures) and a huge **scale model** of the site to bring Polonnaruwa to life. However, many of the most striking relics of the ancient city are in the **National Museum** in Colombo (www.ccf.lk.polonnaruwa).

The Royal Palace ★★★

Only the 3m (10ft) thick lower walls of the Royal Palace survive, but this huge wood and stone structure, built for Parakramabahu I, was originally seven storeys tall. Superb stone lions guard the steps of the **Audience Hall**, next to the palace, where the kings of Polonnaruwa met noble petitioners and foreign envoys. Carved elephants form a frieze around the lower walls, and next to the hall is the **Kumara Pokuna** (Royal Bathing Pool), originally fed by the stream which runs through the grounds.

Nissanka Malla's Palace ★★

This group of ruins, built for Nissanka Malla (1187–96), stands close to the lake and includes a royal bathing pool and a council chamber where the names of royal ministers are carved into the stone columns that once supported its roof.

Siva Devale *

This 13th-century Hindu temple of Shiva dates from the period of South Indian rule which followed the decline of Sinhalese power in the north. Several more devales also date from this era, including two more Siva devales and a Vishnu devale to the north of the Quadrangle complex.

Quadrangle ***

This rectangle of walls encloses the richest collection of ancient buildings in Sri Lanka. In the southeast

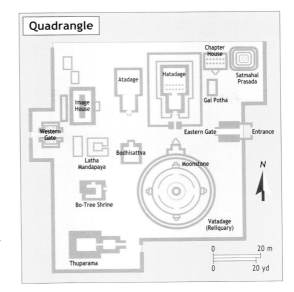

Quadrangle

Chapter House
Satmahal Prasada
Hatadage
Atadage
Gal Potha
Image House
Eastern Gate
Entrance
Western Gate
Bodhisattva
Latha Mandapaya
Moonstone
N
Bo-Tree Shrine
Vatadage (Reliquary)
Thuparama

0   20 m
0   20 yd

ANURADHAPURA AND THE NORTHWEST

corner stands the **Vatadage**, a circular shrine some 18m (59ft) in diameter, housing four seated Buddha images. Next to it stands the **Thuparama**, a fine example of the gedige style of temple architecture which flourished at Polonnaruwa and the only temple with its roof still place. Other key buildings are the **Latha Mandapaya**, a miniature dagoba encircled by carved stone columns and trellises; the **Atadage**, a tooth relic shrine built during the reign of Vijayabahu I; the **Hatadaga**, another tooth reliquary building, from the reign of Nissanka Malla; and the enigmatic, pagoda-like **Satmahal Prasada**.

The Quadrangle's most impressive sight, however, is the **Gal Potha** (Stone Book). This 9m (29ft) slab mimics the palm-leaf books used to record Buddhist texts and royal genealogies, and boasts of the achievements of Nissanka Malla. Northeast of the Quadrangle looms the Parakramabahu Vihara, one of the largest dagobas in Polonnaruwa.

Alahana Pirivena Complex ★★

Scattered for some 6km (4 miles) along the roadside north of the city walls are a number of striking buildings. From south to north, these are:

Rankot Vihara

Part of a monastic college built under Parakramabahu, this 55m (180ft) building is the largest dagoba in Polonnoruwa.

Buddha Seema Pasada

This is the tallest building north of the city walls and was the meeting hall of the monastery complex.

Lankatilaka Gedige

Carved friezes adorn the 17m (56ft) high walls of this huge, roofless temple built in Parakramabahu's reign, which surround a headless Buddha image.

Gal Vihara

Three colossal Buddha images carved from a granite cliff, the tallest of which is 7m (23ft) high, make this important shrine one of Polonnaruwa's most impressive sights.

▲ *Above: Serene Buddha image st the Gal Vihara.*
◀ *Opposite: The huge Lankatilaka Gedige, carved with elaborate friezes, was built by King Parakramabahu.*

POSON FULL MOON

The *Poson* Full Moon Festival **commemorates the arrival of Buddhism** in Sri Lanka in the 3rd century BC and centres on the huge dagoba at Mihintale, where Mahindra, son of the great Indian Buddhist Emperor Ashok, first taught the Buddhist faith to the people of Anuradhapura. There are also religious festivals and processions elsewhere around the island.

ANURADHAPURA AND THE NORTHWEST

Kiri ('White') Vihara

This large shrine survived 700 years of abandonment to the jungle before the rediscovery of Polonnaruwa in the 19th century, and is the best preserved of Sri Lanka's unrestored dagobas.

OFF THE BEATEN TRACK

Between Polonnaruwa and Anuradhapura, several lower-profile ancient religious sites are worth a detour.

Medirigiriya

A circular 8th-century temple, the Mandaligiri Vihara, is the main attraction of this temple site, just outside Medigiriya village and 30km (19 miles) north of Polonnaruwa. Open daily during daylight hours.

Ritigala ★★★

The main attraction at this very ancient site is the **Ritigala Forest Monastery**, built around 307BC by Pandukhabu I on the highest peak in the area, 766m (2490ft) above sea level. About 23km (15 miles) west of Habarana, off A11 highway; open daily, 08:00–18:00.

Mihintale ★

Features of this rock sanctuary about 13km (8 miles) east of Anuradhapura include the Ambasthala Dagoba, at the top of a steep flight of more than 100 steps, and the smaller Hirigaduseya Dagoba, at the summit of the rock. Mihintale's many caves were used by meditating monks, and the sanctuary, built more than 2300 years ago, is thought to be the birthplace of Buddhism in Sri Lanka.

ANURADHAPURA

The jewel of the Cultural Triangle is Anuradhapura, largest and oldest of all Sri Lanka's 'lost cities'. The remains of great palaces and huge dagobas stand beside a 24km (16-mile) **processional avenue** which led through the heart of the great capital. Founded by King Pandukhabaya in 437BC,

THE JETAVANA TREASURES

Archaeologists working at Anuradhapura since 1981 have excavated a treasury of objects from the Jetavanarama complex that have become known as the Jetavana Treasures. They show how far-reaching were Anuradhapura's connections: there are Roman and Indian coins, ceramics from North and West Asia, and fragments of Islamic and Chinese ware. Huge numbers of beads made of clay, glass, stone, and of more precious materials such as gold, silver, ivory and carnelian have also been found, as have intaglio seals made in semiprecious stone and gold, and bronze religious statuettes.

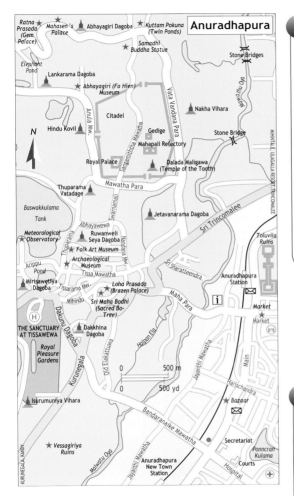

Anuradhapura

Map labels:
Ratna Prasada (Gem Palace), Mahasen's Palace, Abhayagiri Dagoba, Kuttam Pokuna (Twin Ponds), Samadhi Buddha Statue, Stone Bridges, Elephant Pond, Lankarama Dagoba, Abhayagiri (Fa Hien) Museum, Vata Vandana Para, Wana Ahu Oya, Nakha Vihara, Citadel, Anula Mw., Hindu Kovil, Gedige, Stone Bridge, Mahapali Refectory, MIHINTALE, UDAGALA RESORT, TRINCOMALEE, Royal Palace, Dalada Maligawa (Temple of the Tooth), Sagamuttha Mawatha, Thuparama Vatadage, Mawatha Para, Baswakkulama Tank, Swarnamali, Jetavanarama Dagoba, Sri Trincomalee, Meteorological Observatory, Abhayawewa, Ruwanweli Seya Dagoba, Toluvila Ruins, Folk Art Museum, Thuparama, Nandana Mw., Archaeological Museum, Arippu Pond, Tissa Mawatha, Sri Sharatteendra, Mirisawetiya Dagoba, Tissarama Mw., Loha Prasada (Brazen Palace), Mihindu, Anuradhapura Station, Maha Para, Sri Maha Bodhi (Sacred Bo-Tree), Market, Market, THE SANCTUARY AT TISSAWEWA, Dakunu Dagoba, Dakkhina Dagoba, Royal Pleasure Gardens, Dakunu Dagoba, Old Elakattuwa, Halpan Elu, Kurunegala, Isurumuniya Vihara, Harischandra, Bandaranaike Mawatha, Bazaar, Vessagiriya Ruins, Jayanthi Mawatha, Main, Secretariat, KURUNEGALA, KANDY, Malwatu Oya, Jayanthi Mawatha, Anuradhapura New Town Station, Ponncran Kulama, Courts, Hospital

0 500 m
0 500 yd

Anuradhapura was famed throughout the ancient world, and the treasures on display at the Jetavanarama Museum, on site, show evidence of links with the Mediterranean world and China.

For some 1400 years, Anuradhapura was ruled by more than 250 Buddhist and Hindu kings, until it fell to the Tamil

▲ Above: The sacred bodhi tree at Anuradhapura is said to be the oldest historical tree in the world.

invader Rajaraja Chola in the 11th century AD. The Mawathu Oya river separates the old city from modern Anuradhapura, and the ancient buildings stand among **royal pleasure gardens** and ritual **bathing pools**.

Anuradhapura's secular buildings were built partly of wood, so only their lower foundations survive. The giant dagobas, made entirely of earth, brick and stone, still stand complete. The on-site Archaeological Museum contains some of the finds from the site, along with explanatory displays.

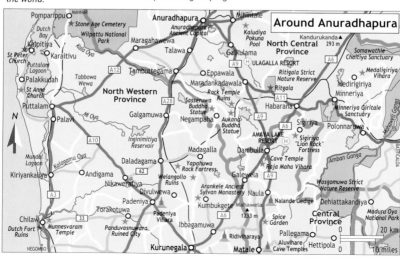

Sri Maha Bodhi (Sacred Bo-Tree) ★★

This huge sacred fig (*Ficus religiosa*) may be the oldest tree in the world. It was a gift from the Buddhist Indian Emperor Ashok in the 3rd century BC, and has been overseen ever since by an uninterrupted series of guardian monks.

Loha Prasada (Brazen Palace) ★★

The stone columns which supported the bronze roof of this once-magnifient building are the only parts still standing. Founded by King Dutugemunu (161–137 BC), it was home to 1000 monks and the entire nine-storey structure was decorated with silver and gems.

Ruwanweli Seya Dagoba ★★★

This 55m (180ft) dagoba is perhaps the most impressive of Anuradhapura's monuments, with its base supported by a ring of carved elephants (most of which are modern restorations).

Thuparama Vatadage ★★

The oldest shrine in Sri Lanka contains the collarbone of the Buddha, given by the Emperor Ashok to Devampiyitissa, the

▲ *Above: The Thuparama Vatadage is the country's oldest shrine and contains the Buddha's collarbone.*

ANURADHAPURA AND THE NORTHWEST

first ruler of Anuradhapura to convert to Buddhism. Although founded in the 3rd century BC, it has often been rebuilt and looks more modern than it is.

Royal Palace *

Next to the ruins of the 12th century AD palace of King Vijayabahu I stand the remains of a temple which once housed the sacred tooth relic which now resides in Kandy.

Jetavanarama Dagoba and Museum ***

Almost 122m (400ft) tall and more than 113m (370ft) across, this shrine is the largest Buddhist building in southern Asia. Next to it, the Jetvanarama Museum houses coins, statues, seals and beads made from precious stones and metals, discovered during the ongoing restoration of the shrine by UNESCO.

Abhayagiri Dagoba ★★★

This 110m (361ft) tall shrine, adorned with carved reliefs of elephants, was built in the 1st century BC and was the heart of a community of 5000 monks. A stone slab north of the building bears what is said to be the Buddha's footprint.

Ratna Prasada (Gem Palace) ★

Only the mighty pillars of this 2nd-century-AD palace, carved with snake spirit symbols, still stand.

Samadhi Buddha Statue ★★★

This image of a seated Buddha dates from the 4th century and is one of Sri Lanka's finest representations of the Buddha.

Isurumuniya Vihara ★★

This 3rd-century-BC rock temple, with its sensual sculptures of embracing couples, is cunningly built into the crevices between huge water-smoothed boulders.

◄ Opposite: The Kuttam Pokuna (Twin Ponds) were used by the monks of Anuradhapura's monasteries.
▼ Below: The Isurumuniya Vihara is noted for its sensual friezes of embracing couples and is one of Anuradhapura's hidden secrets.

WILPATTU NATIONAL PARK

Covering 1100km² (425 sq miles) of jungle and coastline, about 50km (31 miles) west of Anuradhapura, Wilpattu is a refuge for elephant, leopard and sloth bears.

KALPITIYA★★

This village, situated on a narrow peninsula that shelters a string of shallow lagoons, is favoured by kite-surfers and dolphin-watchers, and is a good base for exploring Wilpattu.

ANURADHAPURA AND THE NORTHWEST AT A GLANCE

Best Times to Visit
The northwest is most pleasant from September to late April. From May to September the **southwest monsoon** brings heavy rainfall.

Getting There
By Rail: There are two first-class, air-conditioned ICE express trains daily from Colombo to Anuradhapura, taking just under four hours. There are also two slower second- and third-class trains daily, taking about six hours. There is one express service daily to Polonnaruwa from Colombo, taking just under six hours. Trains to Polonnaruwa continue to Batticaloa, on the east coast. Rail services between Anuradhapura and Jaffna (in northern Sri Lanka) resumed in 2014.
By Bus: Direct buses travel from Colombo to Anuradhapura and Polonnaruwa. There are also direct buses from Kandy to Dambulla, Anuradhapura and Polonnaruwa.

Getting Around
Local buses connect all points in the region. Mini-buses and three-wheelers operate in larger communities. Taxis are available in all towns and large villages (agree the fare before boarding).

Where to Stay
Hotels catering mainly to tour groups can be found at Giritale (strategically located between Polonnaruwa and Sigiriya), Dambulla and elsewhere. Most of the decent budget places are near Polonnaruwa and Anuradhapura, with a rapidly growing choice also of stylish small boutique hotels and jungle retreats, including some of the most prestigious in Sri Lanka.

Habarana
Luxury
Cinnamon Lodge Habarana, tel: 066 227 0011, www.cinnamonhotels.com Recently upgraded resort with great facilities, five restaurants and bars, all in a lush woodland setting.
Sorowwa Resort and Spa, Lake Road, Habarana, tel: 094 66 227 0332, www.sorowwa.com Luxury hotel located next to Habarana's famous historic reservoir – ask for a lake view room for the best experience. The rooms have all the modern conveniences, including air conditioning, satellite television, and beds with orthopaedic mattresses, and the spa offers an extensive range of eastern and western therapies.

Mid-range
Chaaya Village Habarana, tel: 066 227 0047, www.cinnamonhotels.com

A village-style resort with classy bungalows scattered around extensive grounds, infinity pool, good leisure facilities.
Galkadawala Forest Lodge, Galkadawala, Habarana, tel: 077 373 2855, www.galkadawala.com Conscientiously designed eco-lodge sleeping up to 15 people in woodlands where elephants some-times roam, overlooking Galkadawala Tank.

Polonnaruwa Area
Luxury
The Deer Park, Giritale, tel: 027 224 6272, www.deerparksrilanka.com This recently upgraded luxury hotel has swimming pools, spa, tennis court and also a health centre.

Mid-range
Royal Lotus Hotel, Giritale, Polonnaruwa, www.royal-lotus-hotel-polonnaruwa-sri-lanka.en.lk This hotel offers very good value, with air-conditioned rooms, pool, nature walks, wildlife safaris.
The Village, Polonnaruwa, tel: 094 272 222 405, www.thevillagehotel.bookings.lk A comfortable 36-room hotel with air conditioning and a swimming pool.
Hotel Sudu Araliya, New Town, Polonnaruwa, tel: 027 222 5406, www.hotelsuduaraliya.com

Comfortable modern hotel with 50 air-conditioned rooms, bar and restaurant, swimming pool and an Ayurvedic centre. Elephant viewing safaris, boat trips on the lakes, and visits to archaeological sites in the 'Cultural Triangle' can be arranged.

Sigiriya
Luxury
The Elephant Corridor, Sigiriya, tel: 066 228 6950/1, fax: 066 228 6952, www. elephantcorridor.com This superb hotel has 24 luxury suites with private plunge pools and views of Sigiriya fortress.

Hotel Sigiriya, Sigiriya, tel: 066 228 6821, www.serendibleisure.com This most attractively designed modern hotel has very well designed rooms, swimming pool surrounded by attractive gardens, views of the famous rock, and a range of luxurious extras such as Ayurvedic spa treatments.

Mid-range
Sigiriya Village Hotel, PO Box 1, Sigiriya, tel/fax: 066 493 0500, www.forthotels.lk This hotel has a pool, tennis and badminton courts.

Anuradhapura
Luxury
Ulagalla Resort, Thirappane, Anuradhapura,

tel: 011 440 0404, www.ulagallaresorts.com Very stylish villa-style resort located between Anuradhapura and Dambulla, with a chic restaurant, pretty gardens and a host of activities and tours on offer.

Mid-range
The Sanctuary at Tissawewa, Old Puttalam Road, Old Town, Anuradhapura, tel: 025 22 22299. This former colonial resthouse has 16 rooms (only eight are air conditioned), set in attractive gardens. Facilities are limited (no pool or bar) but the restaurant serves good Sri Lankan food and it's arguably worth the price just for the location next to the ancient site.

Budget
Milano Tourist Rest, 569/40 Stage 01, Anuradhapura, tel: 025 222 2364, www.milanotouristrest.com With 16 rooms (all air-conditioned, and some with *en-suite* bathroom), rooftop bar, and two restaurants, this small guesthouse offers outstanding value for money.

Dambulla
Luxury
Thilanka Resort and Spa, 51 Gadawalayaya, Moragollawa, Dambulla, tel: 066 446 8001, www.thilankaresortandspa. com Delightful luxury lodge with great health facilities and activities, set on a hilltop

among gardens and mango orchards.
Amaya Lake Resort, Kandalama, Dambulla, tel: 066 446 1500, www.amaya resorts.com Sybaritic resort and Ayurvedic spa with a fabulous location.

Where to Eat
Generally, the best places to eat are in the hotels listed.

Tours and Excursions
Wildlife and birding trips, 4WD excursions, boat trips and fishing trips on the region's many lakes can be arranged through all the hotels listed here. Many also offer bicycle hire to explore the ancient cities nearby.
Sri Lankan Expeditions, tel: 077 359 5411, www. srilankanexpeditions.com Hot air balloon flights over Dambulla and Kandalama between November and April.
Wilpattu Safari Holidays, tel: 077 3476 288, www. wilpattunationalpark.com Offers jeep tours in the National Park as well as accommodation in a number of lodges and camps.
Red Dot Tours offers a big choice of activities and tours throughout the 'Cultural Triangle', www.reddot tours.com
Sun Rise in Sri Lanka Ballooning, tel: 077 352 2013, www.srilanka ballooning.com Operates balloon trips over Dambulla.

7 Trincomalee, the East Coast and the North

Sri Lanka's last tourism frontier is coming into its own with the end to the tragic civil war, which deterred visitors, developers and investors for more than two decades. This is a region with nowhere to go but up. Its assets include superb beaches, great stretches of forested hills protected by national parks, rich biodiversity, colonial heritage and a climate and culture that is significantly different from that of the rest of Sri Lanka.

Almost one million people live in the 2587km² (1000 sq miles) of the arid Jaffna Peninsula, where dry landscapes are in sharp contrast to the lusher environment further south. Sri Lanka's largest river, the Mahaweli Ganga, flows from its source in the southwest highlands to reach the sea at Koddiyar Bay.

The region is home to a mix of Sri Lankan Tamil, Sinhala and Sri Lankan Muslim people, and there are large Tamil communities along the east coast as well as in the northern Tamil heartland around Jaffna.

The physical and cultural scars of the civil war are still evident in the north. The process of clearing mines and other unexploded munitions from some former combat zones may take up to 30 years. While some Tamil residents of the region have returned to their homes, others remain in exile. However, the end of the conflict has brought about something of a tourism renaissance, especially around Trincomalee and the superb beaches of the east coast, near Batticaloa, at Pottuvil and at Arugam Bay. Meanwhile, the

WARNING

Trincomalee was the Sri Lankan government's main base for military offensives against the LTTE strongholds in the north, and for the final offensive which crushed LTTE resistance in 2009. The LTTE attacked naval and military bases here during the troubles. The city is home to thousands of people driven from their homes by the fighting, and there is still a large military presence here. It is inadvisable to be seen photographing military personnel or buildings, army vehicles, aircraft or naval vessels.

◄ *Opposite: A beach on the East coast.*

TRINCOMALEE, THE EAST COAST AND THE NORTH

The east coast's rainy season is from October to January, with rainfall reaching more than 350mm (14in) in November and December. Rainfall is well below 100mm (4in) from February to July, and slightly above this level in August and September. Maximum temperatures reach almost 35°C (95°F) from April to September, dropping below 30°C (86°F) only for the remaining six months of the year, with an **average temperature** of **26°C–30°C** (79–86°F) all the year round.

region's outstanding national parks – which were virtually off limits to tourists during the more than two decades of conflict, when their jungles provided a refuge for LTTE guerrillas – are newly accessible.

On the east coast, the main towns are Trincomalee and Batticaloa, each standing on a fine natural harbour. South of Batticaloa, the fine surf beaches of Arugam Bay are turning

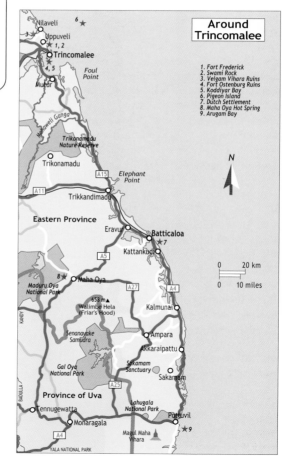

Around Trincomalee

1. Fort Frederick
2. Swami Rock
3. Velgam Vihara Ruins
4. Fort Ostenburg Ruins
5. Koddiyar Bay
6. Pigeon Island
7. Dutch Settlement
8. Maha Oya Hot Spring
9. Arugam Bay

▶ Opposite: Boats on Trincomalee beach.

the Pottuvil area into a hot spot for discerning independent travellers.

Between these hubs, large stretches of coastline are deserted except for small fishing communities, many of which received the full impact of the tsunami of 2004 and were almost completely destroyed. Since then, there has been extensive rebuilding, but work continues.

TRINCOMALEE AND AROUND

Trincomalee has been Sri Lanka's prime gateway to the outside worlds of Asia and the Middle East since the island's early history, and its magnificent natural harbour inevitably drew the attention of the first modern European navigators, who arrived in the 17th century. Occupied successively by the Portuguese, the Dutch, the French and the British during the centuries that followed, by 1795 it had become one of the British Empire's key seaports. Admiral Lord Nelson praised its harbour, Sir Arthur Wellesley (later Duke of Wellington) sojourned here, and during World War II it was the head-quarters of Lord Mountbatten, commander-in-chief of the Allied forces in Southeast Asia.

Few of Trincomalee's pre-colonial buildings survived the successive conquests, but the architecture of the older parts of the city – especially the area around the Inner Harbour – retains a colonial feel, while Fort Frederick, on a promontory jutting northward between Back Bay and Dutch Bay on the city's east shore, is a visible reminder of British imperial power in its heyday. The harbour continued to be a major British naval base for almost 10 years after Sri Lanka

UNDER ATTACK

As a British colony, Ceylon was drawn into World War II in 1941 when, after the Japanese conquest of the British, French and Dutch possessions in Southeast Asia, the island seemed wide open to invasion. The threat never materialized, partly because the Japanese high command overestimated British strength. The British were in fact vastly outnumbered and outgunned at sea and in the air, but despite air battles over Colombo and Trincomalee in April 1942 and the sinking of the aircraft carrier *Hermes* off the east coast, the Japanese did not press the advantage. By 1943 American successes against Japan in the Pacific had removed the threat to the island.

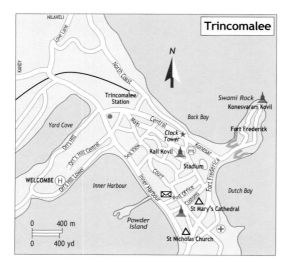

Trincomalee

(map labels: NILAVELI, Love Lane, KANDY, North Coast, Trincomalee Station, Swami Rock, Konesvaram Kovil, Back Bay, Yard Cove, Central, Main, Clock Tower, Fort Frederick, Sea View, Kali Kovil, Konesar, Ort's Hill, Ort's Hill Central, Ort's Hill Lower, WELLCOMBE, Inner Harbour, Court, Inner Harbour, Stadium, Post Office, Customs, Fort Frederick, Dutch Bay, St Mary's Cathedral, Powder Island, St Nicholas Church, 0 400 m, 0 400 yd, N)

gained independence in 1948.

Fort Frederick ★

This still-formidable stronghold was founded by the Portuguese in 1623, then became part of a game of colonial pass-the-parcel which lasted more than 170 years. The Dutch seized it in 1639, then lost it to the French in 1672. Britain took it in 1782, but the French regained it almost immediately, only to hand it back in 1783 under one of the truces that interrupted the almost constant 18th- and 19th-century wars between Britain and France. The British returned it to Dutch rule, but in 1795 (when the Netherlands was allied with France) Britain once again turfed the Dutch out, this time permanently.

The peninsula on which the fort stands is a natural stronghold, made still more impregnable by ramparts and bastions which cross its neck and surround it on all sides. Massive bastions stand either side of the main gate, which bears in stone the English royal motto: 'Dieu et Mon Droit'. Within, it's a mix of colonial-era architecture and more functional garrison buildings.

Wellington House (also called Wellesley Lodge) is claimed to have been the home of Sir Arthur Wellesley during a brief stay at Fort Frederick in 1801 before he went on to India and a legendary military career. Because it is still a military garrison today, Fort Frederick is a sensitive area, and visitors must hand over identity documents and mobile phones to gate guards on entering. Taking photographs within the fort is also inadvisable.

DEEPAVALI

Deepavali, the **Festival of Lights**, is one of the most important festivals of the **Hindu** year. Held in November, it is dedicated to Lakshmi, goddess of wealth and consort of Vishnu. Lakshmi appears with Vishnu in all his reincarnations, and as Sita, wife of Rama, was kidnapped by the demon king of Lanka, starting the great war between gods and demons recounted in the epic *Ramayana*.

Swami Rock ★

On the highest tip of the Fort Frederick peninsula, the modern Thirukonesvaram Isvaram (or Kovil) is dedicated to Lord Shiva and is one of Sri Lanka's most important Hindu shrines. The original temple here was demolished by the Portuguese, but the precinct now houses one of its stone columns and an ancient *lingam* (stone phallus) recovered from the sea bed by underwater archaeologist Mike Wilson.

Kali and Pillaiyar Kovils ★★

West of Fort Frederick's main gate, the Esplanade is another relic of British rule. A broad triangle of parched grass, it encloses a 19th-century cemetery (now very dilapidated). Across Dockyard Road, near the northwestern tip of the triangle, two colourful Hindu temples, the Kali Kovil and the smaller Pillaiyar Kovil, stand side by side, both embellished with gaudy tiers of statuary. Both temples were being restored in 2014 so were not fully open to visitors.

Hoods Tower Museum ★

This museum is yet another reminder of Trinco's historic strategic importance, with three huge naval guns protruding from the walls of an 18th-century watchtower (named for a noted 18th-century British admiral) to command the harbour in all directions. Inside and around the tower is a clutter of military and naval paraphernalia spanning more than two centuries. The museum is inside the Trincomalee Navy Base, and permission is required to enter.

Uppuveli ★★

On the northern outskirts of Trinco (6km/4 miles north of the city centre, easy to get to by taxi or three-wheeler), Uppuveli is a small, tranquil resort with a good sandy beach where fishing boats still share space with holiday-makers. With a handful of hotels (including the best place to stay in the area) and some pleasant restaurants, this is the most suitable place for a longer stay near Trincomalee.

TOURISM AND THE ENVIRONMENT

As in other developing countries, the tourism industry in Sri Lanka has been accused of environmental and social damage. The spread of sex tourism, and the loss of water supplies and access to the sea caused by the building of large resorts, brought criticism from local and international pressure groups. However, continued tension will curb a runaway tourist boom. Damage to the coastal tourism infrastructure caused by the tsunami has created an opportunity for Sri Lanka to rethink its approach. Time will tell whether this will alleviate the problems.

Nilaveli *

Nilaveli has the best beach in the region, but unlike Uppuveli (which is more sheltered) it took the full brunt of the 2004 tsunami. Sooner or later this 4km (2.5-mile) stretch of sand is bound to attract full-scale tourism, but for now it is still a haven for those willing to forgo luxury for peace and quiet. Pigeon Island, just offshore, is a breeding place for the rare blue rock pigeon. Its formerly spectacular coral reef has been severely damaged by climate change and human activity (including dynamite fishing) but still offers good inshore snorkelling.

BATTICALOA AND AROUND

Batticaloa is one of the natural gateways to the east coast, with rail and bus services from Colombo and a coastal road connecting it with Trinco to the north and Pottuvil to the south. It stands on a long, sandy spit, separated from the mainland by a brackish lagoon which extends southwards

▼ Below: Many local people supplement their diet by fishing from the north's uncrowded, palm-fringed beaches, like this angler near Trincomalee.

for many kilometres. Batticaloa was the first Dutch bridgehead during the colonial era (before their ousting of the Portuguese from Trinco) and the grim stone walls of a long-abandoned Dutch fort are a feature of the town centre.

Most of Batticaloa's people are of the Hindu faith, and the town's Periyathambiran Temple is the venue for a colourful festival of music, dance, drama and poetry each year in June. Batticaloa's lagoon is also famed for its quasi-mythical 'singing fish' whose plaintive notes can, so local fishermen claim, can be heard on certain nights. Locally known as 'urikalurukrudu', their numbers seem to have been reduced by the tsunami of 2004, which hit the region hard. Attempts have been made to identify these mysterious marine creatures and to record their 'song', but they remain elusive.

POTTUVIL, ARUGAM BAY AND AROUND

The village of Pottuvil, where the A4 coast highway turns sharply inland, is the gateway to the east coast's most promising tourism hot spot. The **Arugam Bay** area has some fantastic beaches, **world-class surfing**, a lagoon where wild-fowl flock and elephants come to drink, and a rapidly expanding portfolio of pleasant small guesthouses, hotels and beachside restaurants, and vastly improved road access by highways and bridges which have been rebuilt since the 2004 tsunami has made it even more attractive. Rated by some as the third-best surfing spot in the world, 'A-Bay' is also renowned among more up-market and mature travellers. Whether the expected influx of the latter will occur remains to be seen.

Panama *

About 12km (8 miles) south of Arugam Bay, Panama is a small village on a long and spectacular stretch of **golden sand**. The dunes and dazzlingly clear water make it a popular picnic and camping spot.

IRRIGATION

The huge and complex system of tanks, aqueducts, canals and sluices which were built — often using forced labour — under the early Anuradhapura rulers were unrivalled in size and ingenuity anywhere in Asia. Great reservoirs ('tanks') were built by damming the rivers of the dry zone, some of them as much as 64km (40 miles) in circumference. From these reservoirs a network of ever smaller canals and channels fed smaller tanks and eventually rice fields over an immense area covering hundreds of square kilometres.

TRINCOMALEE, THE EAST COAST AND THE NORTH

Lahugala National Park ★

Tiny by comparison with other Sri Lankan wildlife reserves, Lahugala (16km/10 miles west of Pottuvil) is home to a herd of more than 100 elephants, as well as sloth bear, sambar, macaque and other monkeys and the occasional leopard. Its small size means frequent conflict between animals and people living nearby. Electric fences, built by the park authority to protect the crops of the villages bordering the park from being plundered by elephants, have proved ineffective. Lahugala reopened in 2010 after being sporadically closed for security reasons for more than 20 years; ecotourism here is in its infancy, but visits can be arranged through most hotels and guesthouses in Arugam Bay.

Gal Oya National Park ★

Gal Oya embraces 260km² (100 sq miles) of scrub and savannah around the huge Senanayake Samudra reservoir, which was created in the 1950s by damming the Gal Oya

Jaffna and the North

Kankesanturai · Point Pedro · Palali
Karaitivu
Eluvaitivu · Chunnakam · Vallipura Alvar Kovil
Analaitivu · Jaffna · Chavakachcheri
Kayts · Dutch · Kachchai
Nainativu · Fort · Archaeological
Mandaitivu · Museum · Jaffna Lagoon
Punkudutivu
Delft · Maveliturai · Pooneryn · Elephant Pass · Chundikkulam Bird Sanctuary · Chundikkulam
Palaitivu
Devil's Point · Kilinochchi
Erumaitivu · A32
Kakkativu · A35
Iranativu · Kandekal Aru · Mullaittivu
Northern Province · A34
Talaimannar · Per angir Aru · Mankulam · Nedunkeni
Adam's Bridge · Pesalai
Mannar Island · Mannar · Nay Aru · Madhu Road Sanctuary · A9 · Siripura
Giant's Tank Sanctuary · Our Lady of the Holy Rosary Church · Alut Hammillewa
Murunkan · Madhu Road · Vavuniya · Madukanda
N · Pearl Banks · Paraiyanalankulam · Kal Aru · A30 · A14 · Ayiyatigewewa
Tantirimale Ancient Buddhist Monastery · Weddakanda · 121 m · A29
Karaitivu · Wilpattu National Park
PUTTALAM · Medawachchiya · MIHINTALE · Horowupotana

0   20 km
0   10 miles

River. This man-made lake, with its many flooded valleys, cuts almost all the way across the park, and the best way to see its wildlife – including, with luck, its large herds of elephants – is by boat, with trips starting from the small village of Inginiyagala, on the eastern edge of the park. Inginiyagala is about 80km (50 miles) from Pottuvil, off the A25 highway.

▲ *Above: A variety of monkeys can be seen in Lahugala National Park.*

Yala East (Kumana) National Park ★

Yala East is entered from tiny Okanda village, about 32km (20 miles) south of Pottuvil. Surrounding the Kumana Wewa reservoir, this is a region of dry forest, coastal mangrove swamps and lagoons that attract large flocks of waterfowl.

JAFFNA AND THE NORTH

The Jaffna region – heartland of a distinctive Tamil culture – suffered more heavily than any other part of Sri Lanka from the effects of the civil war that raged here for more than 20 years, ending only with the crushing of the LTTE by overwhelming military force. Thousands of civilians died in the army's final offensive of 2008-9 and the task of clearing landmines and unexploded shells from areas where the most intense fighting took place will take decades. There is still a highly visible military presence around the region.

However, Jaffna city, also known as **Yaalpaanam**, is gradually recovering from decades of conflict and is more accessible to visitors than it has been since 1980, with civil air and road transport links restored, and rail service from Colombo to Jaffna was restored in 2014. The flat, arid Jaffna

JAFFNA MUSIC FESTIVAL

Jaffna Music Festival, launched in 2011, features traditional musicians and dancers from all strands of Sri Lankan culture, with performances too from visiting folk artists – in 2011, there were performers from India, Nepal, Palestine and Norway. Funded by the Norwegian Embassy and organised the Sewalanka Foundation and Concerts Norway, the event takes place over the last weekend in March east year.

Peninsula, connected to the mainland by two narrow causeways at Elephant Pass, is strikingly different from the green and hilly landscapes of the rest of Sri Lanka. The lagoons attract a plethora of migrant waterfowl, waders and seabirds. Tourism and business travel are on the increase, and the city's first four-star hotel, a 15-storey edifice complete with rooftop pool, was scheduled to open in January 2015, dramatically changing Jaffna's skyline.

A scattering of gaudy **Hindu temples** lend colour to the otherwise drab and dusty town centre, and a number of large Dutch-era **churches** on and around Main Street are reminders of the town's long-lost colonial prominence.

Jaffna Fort *

The massive star-shaped fort, built by the Dutch, was an SLA redoubt throughout the civil war and was repeatedly attacked by the LTTE. Now open to visitors, it is being restored, but many of its historic buildings have been reduced to rubble.

Kandaswamy Kovil **

On Point Pedro Road in Nallur, 2km (1.3 miles) north of central Jaffna, this is the largest and most spectacularly colourful Hindu temple complex in Sri Lanka, with three towers, covered by a riot of carved and painted deities and demons, overlooking a huge, vaulted prayer hall and a rectangular pool surrounded by a tranquil inner courtyard. The complex is open daily from dawn until dusk.

Offshore Islands **

An archipelago of small islands lies scattered across the Palk Strait, which separates Jaffna from the Indian mainland. Off limits for years, these appeal to only the most curious adventurer, although they have a handful of very dilapidated ruins from different colonial eras, including the ruins of the 19th-century St James Church on Kayts, the closest island to the mainland, and the wreckage of Dutch and Portuguese forts on Karaitivu, the northernmost isle, one of which is

MUDRAS

The hands of each Buddha image are shown in the various *mudras*. These are gestures, or hand positions, with a range of **symbolic meanings**. In the *adhaya mudra*, the right hand of the image is raised to symbolizse protection. In the *vitarka mudra*, the index finger touches the thumb, symbolizing teaching and wisdom, while in the meditative *dhyana mudra* the hands are cupped and resting in the figure's lap.

now a small boutique hotel, and Delft, the furthest island from the mainland, which is also home to herds of wild ponies whose ancestors were brought to the island by the Portuguese.

MANNAR

Mannar Island, a stone's throw from the northwest coast, is linked to the mainland by road and rail bridges. Like all of the north, its tourism prospects have been blighted for decades by conflict. The main town, **Mannar**, faces the mainland at the southern tip of the island, dominated by an impressive Dutch-Portuguese fort. At the island's western tip, the tiny, grubby port of **Talaimannar** was the terminus of a ferry service from Rameswaram, in southern India, which was suspended in 1983. When this edition was updated in 2015 service had not recommenced.

Until the early 20th century, Mannar was famed for its pearl oysters, which grew in huge numbers in the shallow waters all around, including those around the islets of Adam's Bridge, the chain of uninhabited shoals and sandbanks between Mannar and the Indian coast – used by the Hindu god **Hanuman** to cross from India to Lanka in the epic *Ramayana*, and also by the first prehistoric humans to reach Sri Lanka from the mainland. For anyone except for the most determined 'off the beaten track' independent traveller, however, Talaimannar is a bit of a disappointment compared with the rest of the north, with little to see and only the most basic amenities for visitors.

▼ Below: The shallow waters around Jaffna's offshore islands offer rich pickings for local fishermen.

BEST TIME TO VISIT

Monsoon season in the north and east is November–February. The best time to visit is May–September, when the rest of the country is experiencing the south-west monsoon. For **surfers**, April–October is the best time to visit Arugam Bay. **Whale-watching** season is December–April.

GETTING THERE

By air: Fits Air (formerly Expo Air), tel: 011 255 5158, www.fitsair.com, flies several times daily between Colombo and Jaffna.
By rail: Several services daily (plus overnight sleeper trains) from Colombo to Trinco (7–8 hours) and Batticaloa (8 hours). Rail service between Colombo and the north extends only as far as Vavuniya (about 140km/90 miles south of Jaffna), and had not yet been restored when this edition was researched.
By bus: Trinco from Colombo (7 hours), Batticaloa from Colombo (6–7 hours) and local buses along the coast road from Trinco to Pottuvil via Batticaloa. Jaffna from Colombo (8–10 hours). Buses to the north may be stopped at SLA checkpoints.
By sea: Services between Talaimannar and southern India had not yet resumed when this edition was updated for 2015.

GETTING AROUND

Three-wheelers, local buses and taxis operate in and around Trinco and Jaffna and along the coast. Boats operate across Jaffna lagoon and to the outlying islands.

WHERE TO STAY
Trincomalee

Since the end of the civil war, a number of new hotels, large and small, have opened in and around Trincomalee.

Luxury

Maalu Maalu, Pasikuda, tel: 011 738 6386, www.maalu maalu.com Collection of luxurious stylish wooden chalets on the white sand beach at Pasikuda, roughly midway between Trinco and Batticaloa.

Mid-range

Pigeon Island Resort, Nilaveli, tel: 011 230 6600, www.pigeonislandresort. com Delightful small hotel (40 rooms and suites) on an as yet unspoiled beach.

Budget

Aqua Hotel Trincomalee, 42 Alles Garden, tel: 0712 519 749, www.aquahotel trincomalee.com This budget resort on Uppevelli beach offers fishing and boat trips, has a good bar and grill, and its comfortable rooms are excellent value for money.

Arugam Bay
Mid-range – budget

Stardust Beach Hotel, tel: 063 224 8191, www.arugambay.com This hotel is among the best places to stay in Arugam Bay, with a choice of budget cabanas or 'luxury' rooms (at a mid-range price). The hotel has a good open-air restaurant and also offers a range of tours and excursions.
The Danish Villa, tel: 077 695 7936, www.thedanishvilla.com There are five lovely *en-suite* rooms in this establishment, all immaculately designed and decorated, plus a brand new (in 2011) self-contained garden bungalow with two de luxe en-suite air-conditioned bedrooms. The entire place can be rented as a whole.

Budget

Water Music, tel: 063 567 1431, www.watermusic arugambay.com Three *en-suite* thatched caba-nas, plus three cheaper guesthouse-style rooms with shared bathroom, lounge and kitchen. Cook available by arrangement, and in the November–April off season you can rent the whole place.

Jaffna

Jaffna's accommodation scene is changing fast, with the city's first truly international-standard hotel opening in 2015 and changing the city's skyline in the process. However, there are as yet no luxury properties in the region.

Mid-range
Jetwing Yarl Hotel, Old Clock Tower Road, Jaffna, tel: 011 554 5711, www.jetwinghotels.com This 55-room hotel, with facilities including a rooftop pool, is expected to open in 2015.
Tilko Jaffna City Hotel, 70/6 KKS Road, tel: 021 222 5969. www.tilkojaffna.com One of Jaffna's better, more modern hotels with *en-suite*, air-conditioned rooms and facilities including minibar, gym and spa, and internet access. Also has one of Jaffna's better restaurants.
Hotel Lux Etoiles, 34 Chetty Street Lane, Nallur, Jaffna, tel: 021 222 3966, www.luxetoiles.com As of now, the Lux Etoiles is the best place to stay in Jaffna, with eight well-appointed *en-suite* rooms, air conditioning, pool, free internet access and one of the best restaurants in Jaffna.

Budget
Fort Hammenhiel Resort, Karainagar, tel: 011 381 8215, www.forthammenhiel resort.lk This tiny hotel and restaurant by the sea looks out towards the picturesque ruins of a Dutch island fort.

WHERE TO EAT
All the hotels listed in this section have adequate restaurants, and there are also lots of small food stalls and restaurants serving local food to be found on the streets of Trinco, Batticaloa and Jaffna. Arugam Bay has a grow-ing choice of good budget restaurants, serving local food as well as international standards such as pizza and pasta.

TOURS AND EXCURSIONS
Pottuvil Lagoon Eco-Tour, run by a local fishermen's collective, offers outrigger canoe trips on the lagoon. It is situated 2km (1.3 miles) north of Arugam Bay and is home to 70 bird species, crocodiles, giant monitor lizards and monkeys. The tour lasts two hours, and departures are twice daily. Book at the Arugam Bay Hillton guesthouse, tel: 063 224 8189.

National Parks
Four-wheel-drive 'safaris' to the nearby national parks can be arranged through most of the Arugam Bay guesthouses.

Surfing
The Stardust Beach Hotel (*see* Where to Stay) arranges transport to Arugam Bay's top breaks (Pottuvil Point, The Point and Crocodile Rock).

Lanka Surf Trips (tel: 077 624 2795, www.lankasurftrips.com) offers transfers in an air-conditioned minibus with board racks.

Whale-watching
Sri Lanka is on a blue whale and sperm whale migration route, and was a promising whale-watching destination until the waters off Trinco were placed off limits in the 1980s. In 2008, blue whales were seen off Mirissa (between Galle and Matara), and whale-watching trips began from there in 2009. In 2010, whale-watching trips recommenced from Trinco and can be arranged through the **Chaaya Blu Trincomalee** (*see* Where to Stay). **Jetwing Eco** (tel: 011 238 1201, www.jetwingeco.com) and **Nature Odyssey** (tel: 011 230 6421, www.nature odyssey.com) both also offer whale-watching from Mirissa.

USEFUL CONTACTS
When this edition was researched there were no official tourist information offices in Trincomalee, Jaffna, Batticaloa or Arugam Bay. Two websites (www.arugam.info and www.welcometobatticaloa.com) are handy sources of information about beaches, places to stay and activities on the east coast.

Travel Tips

Tourist Information

Sri Lanka Tourism (www.srilanka.travel) is the official national tourist board. It has no overseas offices.

Entry Requirements

Visitors from Britain, other EU nations, Canada, USA, Australia, New Zealand, South Africa and most other countries must have a visa, which can be applied for online at www.eta.gov.lk or bought on arrival. Tourist visas are valid for 30 days but can be renewed in Sri Lanka for a further 60 days. Your passport must be valid for at least six months after the date of your arrival in Sri Lanka.

Customs

You may import one and a half litres (approximately three pints/two bottles) of spirits or two bottles of wine; cigarettes are not allowed duty free. Banned goods include gold; Sri Lanka currency in excess of Rs 250; firearms, explosives or other weapons; antiques; animals, birds or reptiles; tea, rubber and coconut plants; dangerous drugs. Gems, jewellery and 'valuable goods' must be declared on arrival.

Health Requirements

Immunization against hepatitis A, polio and typhoid is recommended. Cholera, dengue fever, rabies and malaria are present. A malaria preventative is recommended especially if travelling during the wet season. Take medical advice before travelling.

Getting There

By Air: Main flight connections from Europe are from London, Frankfurt, Paris, Zurich and Rome to Colombo. SriLankan Airlines also has connections to Delhi, Mumbai (Bombay), Madras, Maldives, Singapore, Bangkok, Kuala Lumpur, Hong Kong, Tokyo and China. Other carriers include Emirates (via Dubai), Royal Jordanian (via Amman), and Qatar Airlines (via Doha).

By Sea: There are, as of 2015, no scheduled ferries between Sri Lanka and India, despite reports that sea services between the two countries would resume following the end of the civil war. A number of cruise lines call at Colombo and Trincomalee on itineraries that combine these ports with stops in India and the Maldives.

What to Pack

For men: light cotton or linen short-sleeved shirts, and/or T-shirts, shorts and light baggy pants for the coast, lightweight linen suit for business or more formal occasions, light jacket or cotton sweatshirt for evenings in Kandy and the hills where evenings can be cooler. Jacket and tie are sometimes required at some older, more formal hotel restaurants and clubs.
For women: linen or cotton skirts, tops, pants; shorts and T-shirts; beachwear. For business, tailored linen dress or suit. Large cotton or silk shawl comes in handy for

cool up-country evenings.
For both: modest wear covering knees, arms and shoulders is required for visiting temples, mosques and sacred sites, including the ancient cities. Other useful items: Swiss Army knife or similar, small torch and batteries, mosquito repellent, binoculars.

Money Matters

The Sri Lankan rupee is divided into 100 cents. Coins come in denominations of 5, 10, 25 and 50 cents and 1, 2, 5 and 10 rupees. Notes are denominated in values of 20, 50, 100, 500, 1000, 2000 and 5000 rupees. Cash can be withdrawn from more than 1000 ATMs throughout the country, provided by branches of People's Bank, Standard Chartered, National Savings Bank, Commercial Bank, Sampath Bank, Bank of Ceylon and others. Most ATMs dispense a maximum of Rs20,000 per day, but some may dispense up to Rs40,000.
Tipping: Universal but modest; a few rupees or even cents in more basic places will be welcomed.

Accommodation

Colombo offers a wide range of accommodation, from international-brand five-star hotels (catering mainly to business travellers) to basic guesthouses. Outside the capital, there are large resort hotels at Negombo, Beruwala and Bentota, and at

Hikkaduwa. Heading around the coast, Galle has several very chic hotels, and along the coast a number of smart boutique properties have opened since the devastation caused by the 2004 tsunami. Hambantota is expected to become a hub for large resort hotel developments following the opening of Sri Lanka's new international airport. Continuing around the coast, there are numerous cheap and cheerful hotels and guesthouses around Arugam Bay, and the stretch of coast from Pottuvil up to Batticaloa seems ripe for development. New hotel projects are also under way in and around Trincomalee and Jaffna, where recovery is continuing following the end of the civil conflict. Inland, there are comfortable hotels in Kandy and close to the ancient cities of Polonnaruwa and Anuradhapura, and an increasing number of stylish resthouses (many of which offer 'meditation retreats', Ayurvedic therapy breaks and yoga sessions). Throughout the country, small family-run guesthouses offer basic but affordable accommodation.

Eating Out

Sri Lanka has plenty of restaurants, ranging from smart Colombo nightspots catering to the country's better off to the simplest of beach bars. At resorts, major hotels usually offer a choice of international-style and Sri

Lankan buffet meals, while around the main hotel complexes at Negombo, Bentota, Beruwala and Hikkaduwa independent restaurants have mushroomed, offering a range of cuisine that reflects the main tourism sources – Britain, Germany, Italy and Switzerland. The main hotels in Colombo have several restaurants each, usually offering Japanese, Sri Lankan, and Euro-international fare. Many smaller, cheaper restaurants around the country offer a choice of Sri Lankan curries and the Sri Lankan version of Chinese rice and noodle dishes like chow mein are re-establishing themselves in the wake of the tsunami. Across the board, restaurant prices are very affordable by international standards, though imported beers and imported wines are expensive.

Transport

Air: Cinnamon Air (tel: 011 247 5475, www.cinnamonair.com), Fits Air (tel: 011 255 5158, www.fitsair.com and Mihin Lanka (tel: 011 200 2255, www.mihinlanka.com) operate a variety of services,

TRAVEL TIPS

(some using floatplanes) from Colombo to most major towns and resorts around Sri Lanka, including Jaffna, Kandy, Trincomalee, Dikwella and Sigiriya. Scheduled routes include Bentota, Kagalla and Dikulla; special charters can also be arranged. Expo Rail (www.exporail.lk) and Rajadhani Express (www.rajadhani.lk) operate private luxury carriages attached to scheduled services on the scenic Colombo-Kandy-Badulla and Colombo-Galle routes.

Trains: Sri Lanka has an extensive rail network and it is possible to get to most of the key places to visit by rail. Some trains offer first, second and third class, some only second and third, some only first and second. In addition, some trains offer air conditioning in first class, while those on the overnight run from Colombo to Badulla offer sleeperettes. Some trains on the highly scenic stretch between Colombo and Kandy have observation car berths.

Buses: State-operated and privately run buses link Colombo with all points and operate between major towns. They are almost always crowded, uncomfortable, and at times dangerous due to minimum maintenance and reckless driving. Rail travel is preferable whenever possible.

Car hire: Self-drive car hire is available but extreme caution should be used when driving on Sri Lanka's roads, due to poor road surfaces. Standards of driving are low and many vehicles, especially buses and lorries, may not be well maintained. Cars with drivers can be hired from travel agencies in Colombo and at resorts, and taxis can be hired by negotiating a daily rate with the driver.

BUSINESS HOURS

Banks normally open 09:00–15:00. Most government and commercial offices open 09:00–17:00. Shops open 08:00 or 09:00 to 19:00 Mon–Fri, closing early afternoon on Saturdays. Most Buddhist and Hindu temples and shrines are open from dawn until nightfall.

TIME DIFFERENCE

GMT +5 hours.

COMMUNICATIONS

Post offices open 08:00–17:00 Mon–Fri. Government post offices exist in all towns and villages and there are also private 'agency' post offices in most larger towns. Telephone calls throughout Sri Lanka are almost all direct dial; if direct dial is not yet available, dial 101 for trunk call connections.

Telecommunication: International Direct Dial (IDD) is available. For international enquiries or operator assistance, tel: 134 For international operator assistance, tel: 100. You can make international direct dial calls and send express mail **faxes**, telegrams and **e-mail** from the new post office at 1st Floor, World Trade Centre East Tower, Colombo 1. Prepaid **telephone cards** can be bought from post offices and shops near telephone boxes.

Mobile phone coverage is adequate across most of the country but is better in Colombo and other major towns. Many hotels and guesthouses offer Wi-Fi internet connection, and there are internet centres in most major towns and resorts.

From	To	Multiply By
Millimetres	Inches	0.0394
Metres	Yards	1.0936
Metres	Feet	3.281
Kilometres	Miles	0.6214
Square kilometres	Square miles	0.386
Hectares	Acres	2.471
Litres	Pints	1.760
Kilograms	Pounds	2.205
Tonnes	Tons	0.984

CONVERSION CHART

To convert Celsius to Fahrenheit: x 9 ÷ 5 + 32

ELECTRICITY
230–240V, 50 cycle AC, three-round-pin sockets.

WEIGHTS AND MEASURES
Sri Lanka uses the metric system of measurement.

HEALTH PRECAUTIONS
You must have comprehensive **health insurance** and take professional medical advice on immunizations several months before travelling to Sri Lanka. Immunizations worth considering include hepatitis A, Japanese encephalitis and typhoid. Malaria prophylaxis is advisable and mosquito repellent is essential. **Do not drink tap water** anywhere in Sri Lanka unless you have boiled or sterilized it yourself. Carry water sterilizing tablets, available from chemists in the UK and elsewhere, if you are heading off the beaten track where bottled drinks may not be available. Food is generally safer than in some other countries in the Asian subcontinent, but you must use your own judgement in deciding whether a restaurant or food stall looks (and smells) acceptably clean. Many travellers in Sri Lanka avoid meat and settle for cooked vegetarian food, which may carry fewer risks. However, Sri Lanka's delicious seafood is hard to resist. Pack Immodium or a similar preparation to alleviate symptoms of diarrhoea, as well as electrolyte mix for rehydration. Sunburn and heat exhaustion are significant risks at all times of year and children, especially, should be kept out of the sun as much as possible. Drink plenty of water to minimize dehydration. Even small cuts and scrapes can become infected. Wash carefully and then apply antiseptic.

HEALTH SERVICES
Most luxury and mid-range hotels have a doctor on call. Your travel insurance should include emergency repatriation. **General Hospital Emergency Services**, 10 Regent Street, Colombo 8, tel: 011 269 1111.

PERSONAL SAFETY
Written permission from the Ministry of Defence is still required for travel to Jaffna, Killinochchi, Manar, Mulaittivu and Vavuniya. Travellers to the north must check the latest security advice before travelling. Do not leave passports, cash, traveller's cheques, tickets or other valuables in your room – carry them with you in a money belt or concealed pouch, or put them in a hotel safe or deposit box. Keep a close watch on your possessions when travelling by public transport. Reporting theft at police stations is a time-consuming bureaucratic process. Use of soft drugs by budget travellers is not uncommon. You may be approached by drug dealers. Be aware that possession of cannabis or other drugs carries heavy penalties.

EMERGENCIES
Police emergency hotline: 118/119.
Ambulance, fire and rescue: 110
Tourist Police: 011 242 1052.

TRAVEL TIPS

ETIQUETTE
Sri Lankans of every faith value modesty. Beachwear is acceptable at beach resorts, but it is less acceptable off the beach and wholly unacceptable at temples, mosques and shrines.

Footwear and headgear must be removed before entering Buddhist or Hindu shrines. Posing for photographs beside religious statues or on top of religious monuments is prohibited. Topless and nude sunbathing are illegal.

LANGUAGE
Sri Lanka is a land of several languages, and language is a political issue. Early attempts at making Sinhalese (or Sinhala) the sole language of government and education sparked the first Tamil protests in the late 1950s. Both Sinhala (spoken by more than 70 per cent of Sri Lankans) and Tamil (spoken by around 20 per cent) now have the status of 'national' languages, while Sinhala is the 'official' language. English, which is widely spoken and used on signs, maps, timetables and place names, provides a neutral link between the two.

SHOPPING
Sri Lanka is a treasure house of riches for the souvenir shopper, with mementoes to suit all budgets. Small craft and souvenir shops surround virtually every resort hotel, and bargaining is the order of the day. At the lower end of the scale, there are carved wooden masks depicting nagas and other mythical characters from the Sri Lankan pantheon of demons and deities. Leather goods such as bags and belts are also good value. The quality and price of silver and gold jewellery depends on the workmanship and the gold and silver content. Precious and semiprecious gemstones are widely sold, especially around Ratnapura, Sri Lanka's 'gem city'. The most valuable are rubies and sapphires. Beware, however, of buying gems on the street or of dealers who offer a seemingly irresistible bargain – more often than not, on returning home, the stone you have bought will turn out to be worth far less than you paid for it, and may be completely worthless. Reputable gem centres in Colombo are the only reliable place to buy stones. Avoid buying goods made from ivory, turtle shell, or reptile skin of any kind. Local vendors may assure you that such wild animal products are legal in Sri Lanka or are made from species which are not endangered. This is unlikely to be true (there are no snake or other reptile farms in Sri Lanka) and your new purchases will be confiscated by customs on your return home.

GOOD READING

Roberts, Karen (1999) *The Flower Boy*, Orion
Clarke, Arthur C, *The View from Serendip*
Ondaatje, Michael, *Running in the Family*, Penguin
Woolf, Leonard (1981) *The Village in the Jungle*, Oxford University Press
Wijeyeratne, Gehan de Silva et al (1997) *Birdwatcher's Guide to Sri Lanka*, Oriental Bird Club

INDEX